QUIET TIME

One Year Daily Devotional for Children in Grades 5~6

Quiet Time
One year daily devotional for children in grades 5-6

Published by Word of Life Local Church Ministries
A division of Word of Life Fellowship, Inc.
Joe Jordan - Executive Director
Don Lough - Director
Jack Wyrtzen & Harry Bollback - Founders
Mike Calhoun - VP of Local Church Ministries

USA
P.O. Box 600
Schroon Lake, NY 12870
1-888-932-5827
talk@wol.org

Canada
RR#8/Owen Sound
ON, Canada N4K 5W4
1-800-461-3503 or (519) 376-3516
lcm@wol.ca

Web Address: www.wol.org

Publisher's Acknowledgements
Writers and Contributors: Betsi Calhoun, Beverly Deck, Amy Speck
Editor: Betsi Calhoun
Project Manager: Tim Filler
Cover Design: Sally Robison
Page layout and design: Sally Robison and Beth Shoultz

ISBN – 978-1-931235-79-2
Printed in the United States of America

name	date	how God answered
....	⬤	....
....	⬤	....
....	⬤	....
....	⬤	....
....	⬤	....
....	⬤	....
....	⬤	....
....	⬤	....
....	⬤	....
....	⬤	....

Missionaries & Church Leaders

....	⬤	....
....	⬤	....
....	⬤	....

I Thank GOD for . . .	*I Praise GOD for . . .*
....	....
....	....
....	....

WEDNESDAY

name	date	how God answered
....	○	....
....	○	....
....	○	....
....	○	....
....	○	....
....	○	....
....	○	....
....	○	....
....	○	....
....	○	....

Missionaries & Church Leaders

	date	
....	○	....
....	○	....
....	○	....

I Thank GOD for . . .	I Praise GOD for . . .
....	....
....	....
....	....

name   date   how God answered

....

....

....

....

....

....

....

....

....

Missionaries & Church Leaders

....

....

....

I Thank GOD for . . .   *I Praise GOD for . . .*

....

....

....

15

FRIDAY

name	date	how God answered
....	⬤	....
....	⬤	....
....	⬤	....
....	⬤	....
....	⬤	....
....	⬤	....
....	⬤	....
....	⬤	....
....	⬤	....
....	⬤	....

Missionaries & Church Leaders

....	⬤	....
....	⬤	....
....	⬤	....

I Thank GOD for . . .	I Praise GOD for . . .
....	....
....	....
....	....

16

FAMILY & FRIENDS   SATURDAY

name   date   how God answered

....

....

....

....

....

....

....

....

....

....

Missionaries & Church Leaders

....

....

....

I Thank GOD for . . .   I Praise GOD for . . .

....

....

....

17

chart your course

Do you ever keep a journal or diary where you write down your thoughts and feelings – and then hope nobody reads it? Well, many of the psalms in the Bible are just that: diary entries from a shepherd-king named David. Each psalm is a musical or poetic prayer to God – written in all kinds of circumstances. Do you have a little notebook where you could write out YOUR prayers to God? **TRY IT!**

MY PRAYER JOURNAL

SUNDAY PSALM 51:1-10

TAKE THE challenge

Have you ever done something wrong and then tried to cover it up? Read how David uncovered his terrible sin in our psalm today.

heck it out!

What words or phrases do you see in these verses that show that David was truly sorry to God for his sin? (Remember – he had committed adultery, lied about it, and murdered a man!) __Have mercy__
__teach me   Surely__ _____

_____

make your choice

Now look at verse ten and write down two requests David asks God to bring about in his life: (1) " __Create__ in me a __pure__ __heart__, O God." (2) " __renew__ a __steadfast__ __spirit__ within me." What does God want to do in my life? __Make the right choices__

MONDAY PSALM 52:1-9

TAKE THE challenge

check it out!

Do you wait until you are CAUGHT to ask forgiveness for your sin?

David's life was very colorful. When the king before him (King Saul) had disobeyed God, David was chosen and anointed by God to be the next king. So King Saul hated David and chased him down and tried to kill him! How does young David describe Saul here? Match the phrases from the verses:

B ___ 1. Did not make God   A. Evil and deceit / falsehood
A ___ 2. Tongue   B. His strength / refuge / stronghold
C ___ 3. Trusted in   C. His riches and great wealth
D ___ 4. Love   D. Like a sharp razor: hurtful

make your Choice

What are two phrases David used to describe himself and his faith?

☐ 1. _an olive tree_
☑ 2. _Florishing in Gods house_

Put a check in the box by the phrase I'd like to describe ME.

TUESDAY PSALM 53:1-6

TAKE THE challenge

check it out!

Have you ever met a true FOOL? What makes a person a "fool" anyway?

Choose the correct answer:

FOOL =

☐ Somebody who's stupid
☐ A mentally challenged person
☒ Someone who doesn't believe in God.

When God looks down on the earth from Heaven, what does He long to find? _peuple Who understand_

Does He find what He's looking for? **NO** / YES (Circle one.)
How many humans are good? _zero_

make your Choice

What can I do to help those who don't believe in God? _____
be a withess

I will pray for _Luke_ (name) to believe in God. 19

WEDNESDAY PSALM 54:1-6

TAKE THE challenge

check it out!

Have you ever been bullied or treated unkindly by other students at school? How does that make you feel?

When David was being bullied and hunted down by Saul's men, he asked God to ___save___ him by His ___name___ (v. 1a). He wanted God to ___hear___ his ___prayer___ (v. 2a) and to listen to his words of hurt. Write out verse 4 here:

" ___Surly God is my help the lord is the one who sustains me___ ."

make your Choice

When others are treating me unfairly or unkindly, what do I need to do first? I always need to remember that G__od__ is my h__elp__.

THURSDAY PSALM 55:1-8

TAKE THE challenge

check it out!

Have you ever felt like everyone is staring at you or talking about you?

How would you describe David's feelings in these verses? ___Very pleading___

He was so upset, what did he wish he could do in verses 6-8? ___that he could fly away___

make your Choice

What is troubling me these days? ___life___

Do I feel "ganged up on" or maybe like I'm going through a difficult trial? YES / NO Maybe I need to ask God who to talk to about my problems.

FRIDAY PSALM 55:15-23

TAKE THE challenge

Have you ever had your best friend turn on you and then even hurt you? Nothing hurts more than a "wound" from a friend.

check it out!

How do you know from verses 12-14 and verse 20 that this psalm was written about a friend who was hurting David? _it says that he betrayed David_

To whom does David go to spill out his hurt and disappointment (vv. 16-17)? _to God_ And what does He do for David? _rescues_ him and _hears_ his voice

make your Choice

God cares so much for me that He wants me to leave all my hurt and disappointment with HIM. He will help me! - Write out verse 22 and see if you can memorize it! "Cast _your burdens to the Lord and he will care for you he will not let the good fall_"

SATURDAY PSALM 56:1-13

TAKE THE challenge

Do you know what the expression "between a rock and a hard place" means? Well, David surely knew!

check it out!

See if you can guess which words from the following list can be used to fill in the blanks in the history lesson below correctly, even if you don't know David's Bio: **Saul - Goliath - scared - land   recognize - forgotten - beard - Lord** (Write out verse 3 on the last line.) **HISTORY 101** David had run to the Philistines' _land_ to hide from _Saul_. He didn't think anyone would _recognize_ him there, especially since he had grown a _beard_. But David had killed a famous Philistine giant there, named _Goliath_. Nobody had _forgotten_ that! David was _scared_ and wrote to the _Lord_: "_when I am afraid I will trust in you_ (v. 3)"

make your Choice

Verse 13 tells me God wants to keep me from falling into sin. I need to "_walk_ before _you_ in the _presence_ of (_your_) _light_." How can I walk in His light of life today? _by making the right decision_

chart your course

David's poetic journal entries became songs the Jewish people sang (and still do today) in worship. "Psalm" actually means "song." David loved music, and while just a shepherd boy, he played the harp (like our guitar today) to pass the hours away.

SUNDAY PSALM 57:1-11

TAKE THE challenge

On the news we see terrible disasters that are happening to people around the world. Has your family ever gone through a disaster or tragedy?

David isn't describing a natural disaster here but one in which he was almost cornered and killed in a cave where he was hiding. Circle the word pictures David uses to describe his predicament. **LIONS - FIRE-BREATHING MEN - RAVENOUS BEASTS - POODLES - MEN WITH SHARP TEETH - TONGUES LIKE SHARP SWORDS - A NET/ TRAP - A DEEP PIT - A WATERFALL - A SINKING SHIP.** David says he will (Cross OUT the wrong answers.): **CRY - FIGHT - SING - AWAKE - HIDE - PRAISE - THROW A FIT - EXALT GOD.**

make your Choice

How will I handle hard things or adversity in my life today?

With a cool head

MONDAY PSALM 58:1-11

check it out!

Do you know what an "imprecatory" psalm is? Find out in today's psalm! (Bet your Mom doesn't know either!)

This is an "imprecatory" psalm of David – one in which the writer is begging God to bring judgment on evil people. As you read David's description of these cruel people, draw sketches of three ways he pictures them here. - Scary, huh?

make your Choice

How did David conclude this psalm of judgment? "_there is a God who judges the ea_ (v. 11)."

Who can I trust with my anger and hatred of injustice in the world? _God_ Will He one day right all wrongs?

YES / NO (Circle one.)

TUESDAY PSALM 59:1-9

TAKE THE challenge

Have you ever said something ugly or unkind and thought nobody heard you?

check it out!

David is still journaling his frustration with his enemies. He asks God to, "_deliver_ me from my _enemies_" (v. 1a) and "_protect_ me from" bloodthirsty men (v. 2b). What kinds of words do his enemies "belch" or "spew" out from their mouths? _bad ones_ (v. 7)

Do they think anyone really hears them? **NO / YES** But what is GOD doing (v. 8)? _laughing and scoffing at them_

make your Choice

When I say ugly, unkind things under my breath, _God_ hears me. What unkind or ungodly words do I need to ask God's forgiveness for? _All the ones I have said at thought x1000_

WEDNESDAY PSALM 60:1-12

TAKE THE challenge

check it out!

Have you ever felt like God has forgotten you or is angry with you? So did David!

David was grieving for God's nation of Israel and its tribal counties. Find the place names (there are eight) from verses 6-8 in the word puzzle:

EPHRAIM, PHILISTIA, MANASSEH, SHECHEM, SUCCOTH, JUDAH, EDOM, MOAB

```
E P H R A I M O H E
D H K S O N O P T L
O I V E N M A H O J
M L S Y K E B A C Y
Z I J O H H D D C H
K S L V Q C L U U A
O T H X N E U J S Q
N I B A K H P U D P
M A N A S S E H D P
```

make your Choice

We know from David's concluding words here that only through _____God_____ can we win our battles and defeat our ____enimies____. I will trust ____God____ to give me victory over my struggles.

THURSDAY PSALM 61:1-8

TAKE THE challenge

check it out!

Have you ever made a special "vow" or commitment to God?

We see David's softer side in this song of love to his Savior. Where did he say he wanted to STAY in verse 4? __in Gods tent and his____ __wings__

He mentions making "vows" to God in verses 5 and 8. A "vow" is a promise or commitment that you make to God.

make your Choice

What have I promised to give God — or do for Him — or never to do again — that I am not keeping? _____ _____ If not, what vow should I think about making to my Savior? __being Godly__

FRIDAY PSALM 62: 1-8

TAKE THE challenge

check it out!

Do you like "rock" music? Well, this song of David's is definitely "rocky"!

As you read through these wonderful verses today, circle every time you see the word "rock" or anything MADE with rocks (i.e. "fortress", "stronghold", "defense", "wall", "refuge") Put the number you count in this box: **9** What do you think it means to have God as your "rock"? _to have him a s g_ _(Foothold of faith)_

make your Choice

When I'm feeling insecure and unsure about life, I can rest in my _f i f e_, the Lord Jesus. I can trust Him with _everything_.

SATURDAY PSALM 63:1-8

TAKE THE challenge

check it out!

Have you ever written a love-song or poem to God telling Him how much He means to you?

Can you match David's feelings with different parts of his life (or Who God is) that he describes here?

MY SOUL -
MY FLESH (BODY) -
MY EYES -
MY LIPS -
MY HANDS -
MY MIND (THOUGHT LIFE) -
GOD'S SHELTERING "WINGS" -
GOD'S RIGHT HAND -

- Seeks God; Sees God in His glory
- Are lifted up in God's name
- Cause me to sing in His shadow
- Longs for God in a very dry land
- Thinks about and remembers God in the night in bed
- Glorify and praise and sing to God
- Upholds me (Holds me up!)
- Thirsts for God

make your Choice

Write a short love-prayer to God on the journal space below:

" _thank you_

chart your course

Bet you didn't know that David was the musician who introduced many new musical instruments into Jewish worship, did you?

DID YOU KNOW . . .

» *That the first INSTRUMENTS mentioned in the Bible were the LYRE and PIPE?*

» *That the biggest BAND was made up of 4000 musicians who served in the temple in David's time?*

» *That the number of SINGERS trained in the temple choir was 288?*

SUNDAY PSALM 64:1-10

TAKE THE challenge

Think of your worst fear. Have you ever actually had to face that situation or event?

check it out!

What three things does David ask God for here, in light of the evil, deadly plans of his enemies?

1) " ___hear___ my voice (me), O God"

2) " ___protect___ my ___life___ from (the) ___threat___ of the enemy"

3) " ___Hide___ me from the (secret) ___conspiracy___ of (the) ___wicked___."

make your Choice

Winston Churchill, famous British leader, once said this, "The only thing to fear is fear itself." David's first request was not, "Protect me from my enemy" but "Protect me from the FEAR (threat) of the enemy." What fear is keeping me from new challenges? ___my reputation___

MONDAY PSALM 65:1-13

TAKE THE challenge

check it out!

What if God had just created everything and then left it to itself, with no controls?

Do the crossword puzzle below, answering these questions from the passage.

Crossword answers:
- 1 (down): blessed
- 2 (across): temple
- 3 (down): joy
- 4 (down): sea
- 5 (across): showers
- 6 (down): sing
- 7 (across): mountains

DOWN
1. The one God chooses to bring near to Himself is this.
3. All the meadows and valleys shout for this.
4. God stills the roaring of this & its waves.
6. The meadows (pastures) and valleys also _____.

ACROSS
2. God's holy house.
5. God softens the earth with these.
7. God formed these by His strength & power.

make your Choice

God not only ____create____s all of nature but He ____help____s it. I can trust His plan for me!

TUESDAY PSALM 66:1-20

TAKE THE challenge

check it out!

Do you know that song, "Our God is an Awesome God"? Today would be a great time to sing it!

The psalmist recounts God's awesome deeds throughout the history of the Jewish nation. Number the following in the order in which they occurred:

4 Brought us into the net/ prison and laid afflictions/burdens on our backs

1 Turned the sea into dry land

2 Saved/preserved our lives and kept our feet from moving or slipping

5 Brought us into a wealthy place of abundance

3 Tried/tested and refined us like silver

make your Choice

David gets more personal in verse 18, where he says that if he regarded or cherished sin/iniquity in his heart the Lord would not ____listened____. What sin might be keeping God from hearing MY prayers? ____all sin____

27

WEDNESDAY PSALM 67:1-7

TAKE THE challenge

check it out!

Did you know that medical surveys have shown that having a grateful spirit (thankful attitude) keeps a person healthier for life?

David asks God to be _gracious_ to him and to cause His _face_ to _shine_ upon them, so that His _ways_ would be made known upon the _nations_. How many times do you count the words "praise" in verses 3-5? | 4 |

make your choice

God wants me to have a ___good___ heart
and a joyful ___soul___ so I can be His
witness on this ___earth___.

THURSDAY PSALM 68:1-10

TAKE THE challenge

check it out!

If you had to describe GOD in five words, what would you say?

1) Count how many times the name "God" appears in these verses. | 12 |

2) Circle two of the things God wants us to do to Him? YELL CRY (SING) (REJOICE) (BE GLAD) (REJOICE)

3) Now write down two things God IS from this passage:

___defender of widows rider of clou___

What do I love most about God? ___his being___
___with me always___

make your choice

28

FRIDAY PSALM 68:11-23

TAKE THE challenge

Do you think there is anything God can't do?

Right in the middle of all these verses about all the powerful things God does on the earth and in the heavens, there is a verse about His personal concern for us. Write out verse 19 in the box below:

check it out!

" _you led captives in your train you recieved gifts from men even from the rebellious that you O Lord God might dwell there_ ." Psalm 68:19

make your Choice

What has God done in my life lately that shows He cares about me personally? _given me many blessings_

_____ I will memorize the verse above, because I need to remember it. **YES** / **NO**

SATURDAY PSALM 68:24-35

TAKE THE challenge

Do you like to go to parades? Have you ever been IN a parade?

Where is the parade (or procession) celebrating God's power going? (See v. 24) the _temple_
Number the participants in the procession according to their order:

check it out!

_2_ the instrumental musicians   _1_ the singers
_3_ the little tribe of Benjamin   _5_ the princes of Judah
_4_ the princes of Zebulon & Naphtali   _6_ the great congregation
_7_ the damsels (maidens) playing timbrels / tambourines

All of them were proclaiming the power, majesty, and strength of the
" _majesty_ of _God_ ."

make your Choice

What is the most powerful thing I've ever seen God do?
work in me

chart your course

Think of all the places and situations from which King David journalled in his lifetime. . .

Shepherding his dad's sheep ~ Psalm 23

Afraid in the land of Philistia ~ Psalm 56

Escaping from King Saul ~ Psalm 59

Getting run out of his own palace by his son ~ Psalm 3

After his big fall into sin ~ Psalm 51

Looking back over all God's blessings ~ Psalm 30

SUNDAY PSALM 69:1-6

TAKE THE challenge

Are you a good swimmer? Have you ever gotten into water over your head and thought you were drowning?

Read verses 1-3 again and draw a picture (stick figure) of David drowning – as described here:

check it out!

He said those who hated him without a good reason outnumbered the ___hairs___ of his ___head___.

In verse 5, he told God that his ___follies___ are (is) not ___hidden___ from Him.

make your choice

The guilt in David's life plus the many enemies who were after him made him feel as if he were ___drowning___ in "deep ___mire___" (v. 2). What "deep waters" am I going through in my life right now? ___camp/hockey___ Who can I hope in? ___God___

MONDAY PSALM 69:13-21

TAKE THE challenge

Have you ever thought about being a LIFEGUARD? See how Jesus is the ultimate lifeguard in today's verses!

check it out!

For what does David pray to the only One Who could rescue him from drowning in his sorrows and troubles? (1) _____answer_____ me with Your salvation. (v. 18b) (2) _____resche_____ me from (out of) the mire (mud). (v. 14a) (3) Don't let me _____sink_____. (v. 14b) What three things did he ask God not to let overflow, engulf, drown, or swallow him up in verse 15?

Floodwaters, _depths_, _pit_

make your Choice

Do verses 19-21 remind you of Someone else Who gave His life for you on Calvary? ___Yes___ Whom do I need to thank for taking my sin and dying to rescue me? ___Jesus___

TUESDAY PSALM 69:22-36

TAKE THE challenge

When someone at school is teasing or bullying you, do you wish bad things would happen to him? Or do you pray for God to work in his life?

check it out!

We see another "imprecatory" (See week two, day two if you've forgotten what this is.) prayer of David against his cruel enemies in verses _22_ through _23_. What does he ask God to do to them in verses 27b-28? "_that them have no agnittance with you_" Do you feel it's OK to pray for bad people not to be saved, but to die in their sins? YES / **NO**

make your Choice

Look up Matthew 5:44 and write down what JESUS tells me to do about my enemies. "_____
_____
_____" Matthew 5:44

WEDNESDAY PSALM 70:1-5

check it out!

When we pray, do we always have to pray long prayers for God to answer us?

This is a short, urgent prayer of David. Let's match up some of these expressions of urgency to God here:

_____ 1. Make haste (Hurry!)
_____ 2. Let those who seek my soul/life
_____ 3. May all who tease me, saying "Aha"
_____ 4. Let all who seek You (God)
_____ 5. All those who love God's salvation should say

A. Be put to shame or ashamed.   **B.** Rejoice and be glad in God.
C. To save or deliver me and help me!   **D.** "Let GOD be magnified / exalted!"
E. Be turned BACK.

make your Choice

Is there something I really need God to do for or in me?
ASK Him right now! He's listening!

THURSDAY PSALM 71:1-8

TAKE THE challenge

check it out!

Do you have a special place you go to be by yourself or to feel protected and secure when things are tough?

Read through this journal entry of David, especially verses 1-7, and write down each phrase or word that tells you where David felt protected and safe.

_____

_____

_____

make your Choice

In verse 3, David says he could _____ go to God for

refuge. When can I go to God for protection and help? _____

_____

32

TAKE THE challenge

check it out!

When was the last time you witnessed to someone – told a friend or family member about Jesus?

Unscramble the three things in this passage that God has given all of us to share and proclaim His greatness. PLIS ___ ___ ___ ___ (v. 23)
THOMU ___ ___ ___ ___ ___ (v. 15)
NOTUGE ___ ___ ___ ___ ___ ___ (V. 24)

Name two things in these verses that David was declaring or proclaiming about God: (1) _____ (v. ____)
(2) _____ (v. ____)

make your ChOice

Who will I purpose (plan) to tell about Jesus and His love today?_____

SATURDAY PSALM 72:1-11

TAKE THE challenge

check it out!

If you were the king of a country, what would you want your subjects to say about your rule?

Most all our psalms to this point have been journalled by King David. Today, though, we are reading the words of King Solomon, David's wise and wealthy son. He is asking God to bless his reign or rule as king of Israel. He tells God that he will be a king who will:

" _____ your (thy) people with (in) _____ ." (v. 2a)
" _____ (to) the _____ of/among the people." (v. 4a)
" _____ the _____ of the needy!" (v. 4b) "Have dominion or rule from _____ to _____ ." (v. 8)

make your ChOice

Some day God may call ME to be a great leader in OUR country. How would I choose to lead or rule others? _____
_____

chart your course

Why not start a prayer journal like David and others? *TELL HIM ABOUT:*

The things that are hard or sad for me

The things that make me glad

What I need help with in my life

Answers to prayer that I can thank Him for

People I want God to help or save

SUNDAY PSALM 72:12-20

TAKE THE challenge

Whom do you know who prays for you regularly?

King Solomon – as he continues to journal the prayer he makes for God's blessing on his reign – promises to d_____ the n_____ who cry out for help, and to have compassion

check it out!

and concern for the poor and needy. He says their _____ is _____ in his sight. He wants to save lives.

make your Choice

In the last part of verse 15, Solomon asks God to let people _____ for him everyday ("continually").

_____ is someone I know who prays for me.

I will call and thank them or write a Thank You note.

34

MONDAY PSALM 73:1-14

TAKE THE challenge

Do you ever wonder why wealthy people - like Hollywood actors and actresses and dishonest people – seem to be so prosperous and rich when they live sinful lives that dishonor God?

check it out!

Perhaps you didn't know that Psalms in the Hebrew Scriptures is actually five books. Our psalm today is the first one in Book Three, and was written by a great musician and choir/band director named Asaph. In verse 3, how did Asaph say he felt about the foolish, sinful – yet prosperous – people in the world? ___I was envious of the arrogent___

What verse reminds us that wicked, arrogant people think God doesn't know about their lives of sin? Verse ___10___

make your Choice

The carefree life of the rich sounds pretty good, doesn't it? (YES)/ NO   And they don't even have to worry about GOD, do they? . . . Or DO they? Find out tomorrow!

TUESDAY PSALM 73:15-28

TAKE THE challenge

Why do you think it's so hard for rich, famous people to come to Jesus and trust in Him?

check it out!

Let's do a little comparison chart here. On the LEFT, write down three things that seem wonderful for the rich and famous. On the RIGHT – put down three things that will end up being true about them when they face God in judgment.

Rich & Famous on Earth (73:4-10)	Rich & Wicked Facing God (73:18-20)
(1)	(1)
(2)	(2)
(3)	(3)

make your Choice

Read over verses 22-26 again, then describe YOUR special relationship with God: _____

_____

WEDNESDAY PSALM 74:1-12

TAKE THE challenge

check it out!

Do you ever feel really "down" or "bummed" about something that has happened . . . only to "come to your senses" later and realize that God is in control and it wasn't as bad as you had thought?

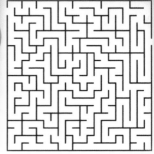

Follow the maze from Asaph's depressed emotions and feelings to his joy in remembering Who God was.

make your Choice

Asaph could have bypassed all his negative emotions by looking to God for help and answers in the FIRST place, couldn't he? - What will I do with my hurt feelings and negative thoughts today?

THURSDAY PSALM 74:13-23

TAKE THE challenge

check it out!

Do you have any teachers at your school who teach the theory of evolution and not the truths of God's creation?

Draw lines between the boxes and squares that match (from verses 12-17 describing God's power over His creation).

	Of the sea monsters/dragons (dinosaurs?)
Divided or split up	The fountain & flood- the springs & streams/torrents
Opened up (did "cleave")	
Broke the heads	The flowing rivers/streams
Broke/crushed the heads	Are yours ("thine")
Made . . .	Of Leviathan, the sea monster
Dried up	All the borders or boundaries of the earth
The Day & Night	The sea
Set/established	Both summer & winter

make your Choice

Who does Asaph say mocks God and His cause "daily" or "all day long"?
_____ Now look up Psalm 14:1
to see what a "fool" is: he is one who says in his heart that there is
____ _____. What "fools" do I need to pray for? _____
_____

36

FRIDAY PSALM 75:1-7

TAKE THE challenge

check it out!

Do you ever try really hard to get your friends or fellow students to notice you and let you be the leader or captain of the group or team?

Check out verses 6 and 7 in this psalm of Asaph. Even though Asaph was the leader or director of all the Israelite choirs in Jerusalem, he says here that promotion (exalting or raising a person to a leadership position) doesn't come from the _____ or _____ or the _____ but ultimately from _____ Who is the _____. He puts or brings one person _____ and exalts or sets up _____.

make your Choice

How do you think God chooses people to be leaders and presidents? What do you think He might look for in a person? _____ _____ Am I the kind of person God could promote to leadership? **YES/ NO** (Circle one.)

SATURDAY PSALM 76:1-12

TAKE THE challenge

check it out!

Think of someone you highly respect and are even a little afraid of because of who they are. Write that person's name here: _____

Today we end our Quiet Time adventure in the Book of Psalms. In our psalm today, Asaph praises God as Judge of all. Write down one descriptive phrase he uses to describe God's power and might here:

_____
_____(v. ___) In verse 11, what does Asaph tell all God's people to do to honor Him as LORD? _____

_____

make your Choice

What promise of commitment can I make to God today — and then keep — to thank Him for being Who He is? _____

_____

God is my _____.

37

wk. 6

weekly passage covered
1 TIMOTHY 1:1-4:8

chart your course

WHO IN THE WORLD WAS TIMOTHY?

 His real name was Timotheus, meaning "Honored of God"!

 Discipled by the great Apostle Paul.

 Had a GREEK dad and a JEWISH mom.

 Probably the youngest preacher ever!

 Maybe his friends called him "Tim."

SUNDAY 1 TIMOTHY 1:1-7

TAKE THE challenge

Do you know any teenagers who like to preach the Gospel?

check it out!

1. Who wrote this letter? _____

2. To whom was it written? "_____, my _____ _____ in the _____"

3. What three godly qualities did Paul start asking God to bless young "Tim" with (v. 2)? _____, _____ and _____

make your Choice

Who could I write an encouraging letter to today? _____
_____

38

MONDAY I TIMOTHY 1:12-17

TAKE THE challenge

check it out!

Have you ever heard a Christian who was involved in great sin share his testimony of how God saved him?

1. Circle the three things Paul admits to being before his salvation: **PERSECUTOR - PASTOR - BLASPHEMER - CAR SALESMAN - VIOLENT/ INJURIOUS - LIFEGUARD**

2. What did he say was poured out abundantly on his life? (Circle it.) **THE GIFTS OF OTHERS - THE GRACE OF GOD - THE OIL OF ANOINTING** What did Paul humbly call himself in verse 16? "The

_____ "

Then he closes with a glorious benediction to God (v. 17).

make your Choice

With whom will I share my testimony of salvation in Christ today? _____

TUESDAY 1 TIMOTHY 2:1-7

TAKE THE challenge

check it out!

How many "prayer warriors" do you know?

List the ways from verse 1 that we should talk to God about others:

_____   _____
_____   _____

According to verse four, WHY does God want us to pray for others? _____

Write the name on the bridge below of the only "mediator" (go-between) between God and man :

MAN

GOD

make your Choice

Two people who really need my prayers today are _____ and _____. Pray for them now.

WEDNESDAY 1 TIMOTHY 2:8-15

TAKE THE challenge

check it out!

What should characterize Christian ladies?

Draw lines from the female below to the qualities that show she is godly.

sexy clothes - faith - the latest fashions - good deeds/works - modest clothing - love - quietly submissive - worships God - always talking loudly - holiness - lots of friends

make your Choice

GIRLS: Pray and ask God to make you a truly godly young lady.
GUYS: Pray and ask God to lead you to a godly wife someday.

THURSDAY 1 TIMOTHY 3:1-7

TAKE THE challenge

check it out!

Do you know the names of the leaders or elders who serve in your church?

X out the things that should not characterize church leaders or elders in a church:

respected   drinks alcohol   divorced

able to teach   self-control   violent

likes to fight   peaceful   unruly

children   loves money   angers easily

What will he fall into (v. 7b) if he is characterized by the negative things above? _____

and the _____

make your Choice

What changes do I need to make in my life so I can serve God in my church someday?

40

FRIDAY 1 TIMOTHY 3:8-16

TAKE THE challenge
check it out!

How do you think a person should behave himself in God's house?

Paul gives qualifications for church deacons here, and then tells "Tim" that he wrote this letter so Timothy would know how folks ought to _____ in God's _____. He calls it "the _____ of the _____ _____" (v. 15). Match (draw lines between) the six things below that Paul uses to describe Christ's godliness:

APPEARED / MANIFESTED -   - BY ANGELS
VINDICATED / JUSTIFIED -   - IN THE WORLD
SEEN -   - IN A BODY/ THE FLESH
PREACHED / PROCLAIMED -   - AMONG THE NATIONS
BELIEVED ON -   - BY THE SPIRIT
TAKEN UP -   - INTO GLORY

make your Choice

Is there something I do in church that I shouldn't? **YES/ NO**

What do I need to change about my behavior? _____

SATURDAY 1 TIMOTHY 4:1-8

TAKE THE challenge
check it out!

What kind of physical training are you involved in? Are you a runner or biker or maybe a roller blader?

Paul warns "Tim" that in later times some people will abandon (depart from) the _____ and listen to (heed or follow) _____ spirits and doctrines of (things taught by) _____ instead of GOD'S TRUTH! He says that Timothy would be a _____ _____ of Jesus Christ if he pointed these untruths out to his Christian brothers. He then instructs young Timothy that training in (circle one) **GODLINESS / ATHLETICS** is much more important than training in **GODLINESS / ATHLETICS** (circle one).

make your Choice

Which is more important? (Check the box.)

☐ My sports team practices

☐ Having my Quiet Time in God's Word

41

chart your course

DID YOU KNOW . . .

Maybe his friends called him "Tim."

Probably the youngest preacher ever!

Had a GREEK dad and a JEWISH mom.

Discipled by the great Apostle Paul.

His real name was Timotheus, meaning "Honored of God"!

SUNDAY 1 TIMOTHY 4:9-16

TAKE THE challenge

Who's the best example of a godly Christian you know?

Paul told Timothy, "Don't let **ANY**one look down on ("despise") you because you are (circle one): FROM A MIXED MARRIAGE - UNKIND - TOO SHORT - SO YOUNG   "Tim" is instructed to _____ an _____ to other believers in what five important areas? List them on the lines below.

check it out!

☐ _____ ☐ _____

☐ _____ ☐ _____

☐ _____

make your Choice

In one of the boxes above, check the area I most need to work on in order to be a good example or testimony to others. Now ask God to help you.

MONDAY 1 TIMOTHY 5:1-8

TAKE THE challenge

check it out!

How do you show your grandparents you love them?

Match (draw lines between) the kinds of people Paul instructs Timothy about with the way they should be treated.

Elderly men	**As sisters**
Younger men	**Honor them with recognition**
Elderly women	**Like fathers**
Widows	**Like mothers**
Younger women	**As brothers**
One's own family or relatives	**Provide for their needs**

make your choice

Do something kind to help an elderly shut-in or neighbor today.

I will _____

_____

TUESDAY 1 TIMOTHY 5:9-16

TAKE THE challenge

check it out!

What do you think qualifies a widow for financial help or aid from the church?

Timothy was being instructed about the widows of the church. A widow was not to qualify for financial aid unless she was over 60, faithful to one _____ and well _____ for her _____ _____. List at least three good deeds or works for which she was to be known.

1) _____

2) _____

3) _____

make your choice

Think of a widow in your church or community and pray especially for her today. Her name is _____

_____.

TAKE THE challenge

check it out!

Can you name two leaders or pastors of your church?

This is a passage of practical pastoral instruction for Timothy. It deals with _____ who rule _____ being paid by the church. Then Timothy is told NOT to show favoritism to certain people. But the very best advice Paul gives him is at the end of verse 22: "_____ _____."

make your Choice

Do any shows I watch on T.V. or songs I listen to cause me to think impure or sinful thoughts? **YES / NO** What will help me stay PURE? _____ _____

TAKE THE challenge

check it out!

What is one thing you don't have that you wish you did?

Here Paul addresses proper behavior as a Christian slave or employee (vv. 1-2) and how to identify and deal with a false teacher (vv. 3-5). He says the false teacher thinks that financial gain equals g_____ (v. 5c). Then he goes on to share a very important principle:

G _ _ _ _ _ _ _ _ _ _

+

C _ _ _ _ _ _ _ _ _ _ _ _ _

=

G _ _ _ _ _

G _ _ _ _

make your Choice

Think of that thing you wish you had. Can you take it to Heaven with you? **YES/NO** Does it only meet a "NOW" need or an ETERNAL need? _____ The opposite of being CONTENT with what I have is being COVETOUS! I will choose to be _____ today.

FRIDAY 1 TIMOTHY 6:9-16

TAKE THE challenge

check it out!

What would you start doing differently if you knew Jesus was coming back next week?

Paul wanted his son in the faith to live a life he'd be glad he'd lived when Jesus comes back. Finish his last special instructions below: → F __ __ __ the love of money. ~ Follow after (pursue) : _____, _____, _____, _____, and _____. → F _____ the good _____ of _____. → _____ _____ of/on e_____ l_____.

make your Choice

What would I be ashamed of in my life if Jesus came back today? _____

SATURDAY 1 TIMOTHY 6:17-21

TAKE THE challenge

check it out!

Did you ever wish you were really, really rich?

Pastor Timothy must have had some wealthy people in his church. What are two things he needed to warn them about: (1) Don't be _____ _____ (v. 17). (2) Put your _____ only in God, not uncertain riches (v. 17). (3) This is what you SHOULD be doing with all your money (v. 18): _____, be _____ in good _____, and be willing to share generously!

make your Choice

What do I do with money when I get it? _____
Do I ask God whom I can help with that money? _____
_____

45

chart your course

What do the following words have in common?

GLEANING: To gather grain left behind by reapers

WIZARD: a person who practices magic; magician or sorcerer

MEDIUM: a person through whom the spirits of the dead are alleged (suspected) to be able to contact the living

So, what do they have in common? They are all found in the passages of God's Word that we will be studying this week. Watch for them!

SUNDAY — LEVITICUS 1:1-9

TAKE THE Challenge

check it out!

When in doubt, follow the directions!

God gave Moses some specific instructions for the Israelites to follow when they offered a sacrifice for their sins. Read the verses from today's passage and match these instructions below:

Verse 3: They were to offer a "male without" what?

Wood

Verse 4: The person was to "lay his hand(s)" on what?

Defect/blemish

Verse 5: After he kills the bull, Aaron's sons, the priests bring (present) what?

Pieces of the animal including its head

Verse 7: Aaron's sons then put fire on the altar and arrange (or lay) what?

The blood

make your Choice

Jesus gives me some specific instructions about what to do when I sin too! I John 1:9 says I must: (Circle one) WAIL AND CRY - LIGHT CANDLES - CONFESS MY SIN - GO TO CHURCH A LOT. and then Jesus will: (Circle one) FORGIVE MY SIN - TURN HIS BACK ON ME - GIVE ME EXTRA CREDIT.

MONDAY LEVITICUS 5:3-4

TAKE THE challenge

check it out!

It wasn't me! I didn't do it on purpose!

Have you ever said those words? When God gave the Israelites instructions on how to deal with their sin, He even included sins they did not do on purpose. Today's Bible reading tells us how the Israelites were to react when they found out about (knew about or were made aware of) their sin. Unscramble the word in verse 3 and 4 that tells you this:

TUIGLY _____

make your Choice

How do I react when someone accuses me of doing wrong? Do I take the blame and ask forgiveness when my parents, teachers or leaders explain that I DID do something wrong? _____
Do I have a good attitude and a cheerful spirit afterwards? _____
Whom can I ask to help me to do right every day? _____

TUESDAY LEVITICUS 17:1-14

TAKE THE challenge

check it out!

Where's the life?

The question above is answered twice in this passage. Look closely at the picture below and find the letters of the word that will finish this sentence. The life of the creature (or flesh) is in the
_ _ _ _ _. In verse 11, God says that it is the
_____ that makes an _____ for
one's life or soul. "Atonement" is the act of God in which He reestablishes a sinful person's relationship with Himself through a blood sacrifice.

make your Choice

Jesus was my blood sacrifice on the cross so that I could have eternal
_ _ _ _. He shed his b __ __ __ __ so that I could have
my __ __ __ __ forgiven. I will take time right now to thank Him
in prayer for giving His blood for me so that I can have life!

47

WEDNESDAY LEVITICUS 19:9-18

check it out!

Don't forget to share!

How was an Israelite farmer to provide for the poor in vv. 9 and 10? They were not to go right to the _____ of the field and they were to leave the g_____ (leftovers).

This means that poor people could come after the fields were harvested and get what was left over.

make your Choice

How am I at sharing? Do I WILLINGLY share with those who ask me? **YES / NO** Is there someone I can think of with whom I could share money? (Maybe a missionary or a friend who does not have much?) _____ Maybe the next time I buy candy, I could buy some JUST TO SHARE. I will ask God right now to show me how I can share with others.

THURSDAY LEVITICUS 20:6-10; 22-27

check it out!

OUIJA do it?

In vv. 6 and 27 God uses pretty strong language to describe what will happen to the person who turns to mediums (see Chart Your Course), spiritists, or wizards to get advice or to find out about the future. Sometimes you may not even know that you have stepped in Satan's territory with things like tarot cards, fortune telling, or Ouija boards. In v. 6, God says He will "c __ __ o __ __ from His people" anyone involved in these practices.

make your Choice

Satan is very sneaky. He may get you to think that the things listed above are harmless . . . but anything to do with the devil is always dangerous! Can I think of something that I have done that is not pleasing to God? _____ I will ask forgiveness right now, and ask God to help me to turn away from that sin for good.

FRIDAY LEVITICUS 22:17-25

TAKE THE challenge

check it out!

100% Perfect... Nothing Less!

As you read the verses today, what did you notice? Every animal that was used as a sacrifice to the Lord had to be perfect. The Lord Jesus was able to take the punishment for my sin because He is **YLOH** and **TCEFREP**. (These words are backwards: unscramble them and write them here.) _____ and _____.

make your Choice

Am I trying to be like Jesus when I'm at church? Circle all that apply: Do I ..... LISTEN WITHOUT SQUIRMING PAY ATTENTION SING HEARTILY FOLLOW ALONG IN MY BIBLE ACT RESPECTFULLY GO CHEERFULLY GIVE GENEROUSLY? If I did not circle some of these, why is that? I will remember to try to be like Jesus this week at church and at home.

SATURDAY LEVITICUS 23:4-14

TAKE THE challenge

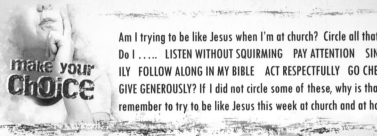

Feasts to Remember

In these verses, the Lord is giving guidelines to the Israelites about when to hold feasts that will help them remember God's faithfulness to them. Can you unscramble the three feasts described in these verses?
SIRIFFRUTTS _ _ _ _ _ _ _ _ _ _ _
SAVEPROS _ _ _ _ _ _ _ _
LEANUDEVEN DRABE _ _ _ _ _ _ _ _ _ _ _
_ _ _ _ _

check it out!

Why did He want them to have these special days of remembrance? Because sometimes we are quick to forget how much we have to be thankful for.

make your Choice

Can I think of something that God has done for me that I want to forget?_____

Lord, I thank you today for _____,

_____, and _____. 49

chart your course

Did you know that trumpets mentioned in the Old Testament were often made from ram's horns? Some of the more special trumpets were made from beaten silver. Trumpets were used to signal many events, including the beginning of each month, as well as the start of festivals.

SUNDAY LEVITICUS 23:15-22

TAKE THE challenge

The Numbers Game!

check it out!

Let's add up the numbers in today's passage!

v. 15 _____ Sabbaths (weeks)

v. 16 _____ days

v. 17 _____ loaves

v. 18 _____ lambs (without blemish or defect)

v. 18 _____ young bull

v. 18 _____ rams

v. 19 _____ goat and

v. 19 _____ lambs (less than one year old)

= _____ Total

These numbers help us know what happened during the "Feast of Weeks," a one day festival that the people of Israel celebrated to praise God for a bountiful harvest. What were the people not supposed to do during this time? (See v. 21.)

_____

make your Choice

Just like above, I can add up the bountiful blessings in my life! What are some things I want to thank and praise God for today?

_____, _____,

_____

TAKE THE challenge

check it out!

A day of rest for you!

In today's passage, we read about two holidays that the Israelites were to celebrate: The Feast of Trumpets and the Day of Atonement. Look in the word search to find words associated with these special days. What is one word in the puzzle that God commanded the people NOT to do on these special days? _____

```
H Y G F A I W O R K
T F S O T P P O E X
A H I R O C F M U V
B O M R N F A E X R
B L S T E P M U R T
A Y L R M D R Z S E
S M I G E N X E D W
E N R E N Z R E U Q
G K Q J T F Y U A H
A U N L V R E S T M
```

ATONEMENT   FIRE
HOLY   OFFERING
REST   SABBATH
TRUMPETS   WORK

make your Choice

What is my favorite holiday? _____

What does that special day remind me about God? _____

_____

TAKE THE challenge

check it out!

A week of contagious joy and praise!

The Feast of Tabernacles is described in this passage today. Crack the code to find out the purpose of all these feasts and celebrations. They were to remind the Israelites:

CODE: A=1 D=2 E=3 F=4 G=5 H=6 I=7 L=8 N=9
      O=10 P=11 R=12 S=13 T=14 W=15

&
15 6 10   5 10 2   7 13   15 6 1 14   6 3   6 1 13

2 10 9 3   4 10 12   6 7 13   11 3 10 11 8 3

make your Choice

What do I know about God? He is ... _____

What is something amazing He has done for me recently?

_____ I will take time right

now to thank God for Who He is and what He has done for me!   51

WEDNESDAY LEVITICUS 25:1-17

TAKE THE challenge

check it out!

Give the land a break!

In today's passage, God instructs the Israelites to plant their fields and work hard for how many years? (v. 3) _____ What are they to do during the next year? _____

How will they live during this time? _____

_____

make your Choice

God wants to see us work hard at the things we are supposed to be doing — like: CHORES MY PARENTS ASSIGN ME - SCHOOL WORK - KEEPING THE ENVIRONMENT CLEAN - MY SPORTS PRACTICES - MUSIC LESSONS. But He also wants me to take a special rest each week. My "seventh" day of rest is _____

THURSDAY LEVITICUS 26:3-17

TAKE THE challenge

check it out!

Will you obey?

In vv. 4 -12, God tells the Israelites the things that He will do for them if they obey Him. Unscramble two of the blessings of <u>OBEDIENCE</u> that are found in: v. 4 AINR __ __ __ __

v. 6 EACPE __ __ __ __ __

<u>DISOBEDIENCE:</u>

v. 16 RRRTEO __ __ __ __ __ __

v. 17 MNESIEE __ __ __ __ __ __ __

make your Choice

I have a choice each day to obey or disobey God's Word. What is one area of my life that I am not as obedient in as I should be?

_____

I will pray right now and ask God to help me to be more obedient

to Him in this area.

FRIDAY — LEVITICUS 26:18-31

Will you listen?

Wow! Our obedience is REALLY important to God. What does God say keeps us from listening to Him in verse 19? The definition of this word is "having or displaying excessive self-esteem," or "having an assumed superiority or loftiness." In verses 20–31, look at all the terrible things that will result from a prideful attitude. Write at least two of these down on the lines provided:

_____

_____

Think for a minute… Am I a proud person? NO / YES / SOMETIMES
Do I try to work things out on my own instead of listening to God and asking Him for help? NO / YES / SOMETIMES
What can I do to work on this? _____

_____

SATURDAY — LEVITICUS 26:32-46

A-maze-ing!

START

God gave all these decrees and laws to Moses for the Israelites on what mountain (v. 46)? Mt. _____.
Do the following maze to lead Moses from the mountain back to the Israelites.

FINISH

In v. 45 God says He brought the Israelites out of Egypt to be "their God." Is God my God? Can I remember a time when I asked Jesus to be my Savior from sin? When was it? _____
Who was with me? _____ How did I feel? _____

53

chart your course

How would you like to live in the desert, eat grasshoppers, and wear clothes made of camel skin? How would you like to spend a day with Jesus, watching what He does? This week, you'll find out!

SUNDAY MARK 1:1-13

TAKE THE challenge

What not to wear?!?

check it out!

Look at v. 6. How is John the Baptist's wardrobe described? He wore clothes made of _____ and a belt made of _____.

He also ate odd things that we wouldn't think of eating today! He ate _____ and _____.

make your Choice

John's message was that Jesus was greater than he was. How do I treat Jesus? Do I give Him the honor He deserves? _____

What ways might I be showing disrespect for Jesus? (i.e.: taking God's name in vain by saying "Oh, my god!") _____

_____

TAKE THE challenge

check it out!

Four men and a spirit!

In today's passage, Jesus calls four of His disciples to follow Him. What were the men doing when Jesus called them? _____ Write their names here: S_____, A_____, J_____, and J_____. Jesus also heals a man indwelt by an evil spirit (or demon). This evil spirit knew immediately who Jesus was! What did he proclaim about Jesus at the end of v. 24? "_____

_____"

make your Choice

Who do I say that Jesus is? Is He my Savior? YES/ NO   If yes, then His Spirit indwells you and Satan's evil spirits cannot dwell in you or hurt you. That's good news, huh? If I don't know Jesus as my Savior, then I should talk to my parents, leader, or teacher about how to invite Him into my life.

TAKE THE challenge

check it out!

When should I spend time with God?

Verse 35 tells us when Jesus spent time with God, His Father. Circle the time Jesus met with God:

Late at night   *In the afternoon*
Very early in the morning
After supper   *At lunchtime*

What are some of the things He had done the day before? (vv. 29-34) _____
Don't you think He would have been pretty tired after all that? _____ But He STILL got up _____ to meet God!

make your Choice

When do I normally do my quiet time? Write the time on the clock face below. Is this the time when I can give my best to God? YES/NO If no, when would be a better time for me to meet with God?

_____

55

WEDNESDAY MARK 1:36-45

TAKE THE challenge

check it out!

Can you keep a secret?

Jesus healed a man of _____ in v. 41, but then gave him this warning in v. 44: " _____ _____ _____." Look at v. 45. Did the man obey Jesus? _____

Why do you think it was so hard for this man to keep quiet? _____

What happened when people found out what Jesus had done for the man?_____

make your Choice

How would I feel if I were cured from this horrible contagious disease of leprosy? _____ What would I want to tell people?_____ Whom would I want to praise?_____ SIN is more horrible than the disease of leprosy, because it separates me from God. If I am saved, I have been delivered from my_____!

THURSDAY MARK 2:1-12

Can't get in? Go through the roof!

TAKE THE challenge

check it out!

Four friends helped their sick friend get to see Jesus. Find words about this story in the puzzle:

```
E P H R A I M O H E
D F K S O N O P T D
C A P E R N A U M E
M I S Y O H B A C Z
Z T D R O W F D C A
K H P V M E O U U M
O A H X N H O J S A
C N E V I G R O F P
```

Write down the wonderful words Jesus said to the paralyzed man when He saw his faith (v. 5b):

CAPERNAUM, ROOM, WORD, ROOF, FAITH, FORGIVEN, SON, AMAZED

_____, _____ _____
_____ _____ (thee)."

make your Choice

How can I help my friend get to Jesus? Circle all that apply:
Talk about Jesus — Invite my friend to church or Olympians — Pray for my friend — Be kind to my friend — Give them a gospel tract — Eat spaghetti with my friend. - *Lord Jesus, please give me the courage to share You and Your healing love with a friend who doesn't know You.*

TAKE THE challenge

check it out!

Who needs a doctor?

What reason did Jesus give in v. 17 for eating with tax collectors and sinners? "_____

_____

_____"

Jesus said He came to call _____

to repentance and faith in Him? How many people are sinners?

_____ (If you're not sure, check out Romans 3:23.)

make your Choice

Sometimes people confuse being religious with being righteous. Circle the ONLY way I can become righteous: by being good - by going to church - by saying many prayers — by trusting in Jesus to forgive my sin. (Hint: The last answer is the right one!)

TAKE THE challenge

check it out!

Strange happenings, miraculous events!

The crowd was so big and so pressing that Jesus had to get into a __ __ __ __ to be able to teach and heal the people that were sick! Verse 11 tells us what other strange events kept happening that day: Unclean or evil spirits would _____

and yell "_____."

What did Jesus command the spirits not to tell? _____

_____.

make your Choice

If I know Jesus as my Savior, He gives me a command in Mark 5:19 that is the opposite of this command. Write Mark 5:19 here:

"_____

_____"

scheming enemies

chart your course

What happens?
Who is Legion?
Dive into God's
Word this week!

parables

evil spirits

a great storm

SUNDAY MARK 3:13-21

TAKE THE challenge

Who were Jesus' special friends?

Jesus called twelve men to work with Him closely while He lived on earth. He even gave two of them a nickname! See if you can get the clues and fit all twelve disciples into the crossword puzzle below.

check it out!

DOWN
1. Brother of James
2. _ _ _ D D A E _ _ _ _
5. B _ _ _ _ _ _ _ _ _ _ W
8. The "publican" or tax collector (See Matt. 9:9.)
12. Son of Alphaeus

ACROSS
3. T _ _ M _ S
4. He betrayed Jesus.
6. A _ _ _ _ E W
7. The zealot, Canaanite or "zelotes"
9. Called Simon at first
10. P H _ _ _ P
11. Son of Zebedee

make your Choice

If I follow Jesus as my Savior and Lord, I am His disciple too! How can I show Jesus that I love Him today? _____

_____

58

MONDAY MARK 3:22-35

TAKE THE Challenge

check it out!

Math in the Bible?

Do you like math? This passage is almost like doing math! See if you can find the answers below:

v. 24 – A kingdom ÷ a kingdom (itself) = cannot

_____

v. 25 A house ÷ itself = cannot _____

v. 26 Satan ÷ Satan = He cannot _____

What does all this mean? The Pharisees were accusing Jesus of doing miracles by the power of Satan. Jesus refuted their argument and showed them how silly it was by the "math problems" above. In other words, Jesus' power had to come from God for Him to be able to cast out Satan and heal people of their diseases.

make your Choice

Do I believe that Jesus' power comes from God and that Jesus is the Son of God? If yes, I have His power by the Holy Spirit living within me to help me each day. These are ways I need the Holy Spirit to help me today: **be bold for God - obey my parents - speak kind words - watch only good TV programs - Other:** _____

TUESDAY MARK 4:1-20

TAKE THE Challenge

check it out!

What kind of soil are you?

Read today's passage and then finish filling in the chart. The seed is the W _ _ _ . (v.14)

KIND OF SOIL	WHAT HAPPENED	WHAT IT MEANS
Fell along path v. 4		Satan takes away the Word when heard.
Rocky places vv. 5-6		Hears the Word & receives with joy, but lasts a short time
Thorny soil v. 7		Hears the Word but worries and wealth choke the Word
Good soil v. 8		Hears & accepts the Word & produces lasting fruit

make your Choice

Read the finished chart and ask: What kind of soil am I? _____

_____ Why? _____

_____

59

WEDNESDAY MARK 4:21-34

TAKE THE challenge
check it out!

The hidden lamp

If you had a bright new lamp, would you want to hide it under a bowl or under your bed? NO! Where would you want to put it? _____ _____ Since we know Jesus, He wants us to show our faith in Him to others!

make your Choice

What are some ways that I can show others that I belong to Jesus? _____ _____

Who can I pray for that they'll see Jesus in my life? _____ _____

THURSDAY MARK 4:35-41

TAKE THE challenge
check it out!

Are you afraid?

Pretend that you are a reporter giving the facts about today's passage:

Where were the disciples? _____

Why were they afraid? _____

How big were the waves? _____

What was Jesus doing? _____

What did the disciples do? _____

What did Jesus do? _____

How did the disciples react? _____

make your Choice

The disciples had been with Jesus when He performed many miracles, yet they were still afraid of this big storm! What prayer of mine has Jesus answered recently? _____

How can I remember to trust Jesus in the future? _____

FRIDAY MARK 5:1-10

TAKE THE challenge

check it out!

Talk about the HULK!!

Think of the strongest person you know or have read about, real or pretend, and draw him below.

Now draw a jail around your strong man, because even though the man in today's passage was so strong that he could break chains, it was as if he were living in a prison because of the evil spirits living inside him. Who can rescue him?

make your Choice

Sometimes I might feel like I am caught in a prison of my sin, and I can't stop. Who can help me to escape my self-made jail of sin? _____ My "sin-jail" is _____.

I will pray right now for Jesus to help me stop this sin.

SATURDAY MARK 5:11-20

TAKE THE challenge

check it out!

Who is stronger than the strongest Superhero??

Where did Legion want Jesus to send them? v.11

_____

How many pigs were there? _____ (v. 13)

What happened to them? _____

_____ (v. 13)

What happened to the strong man in v. 15? _____

_____

make your Choice

What am I afraid of? _____

How can Jesus help me conquer my fears? _____

_____ Check out 1 John 4:4, a really great promise to me if I know Jesus!

chart your course

A woman suffered for twelve years – HEALED!

A twelve year old girl, DEAD – THEN ALIVE!

Five THOUSAND people – FED with a small lunch!

Jesus' miraculous works continue this week!

SUNDAY MARK 5:21-34

TAKE THE challenge

Who can help me?

check it out!

Two people needed Jesus' help in today's passage.

Who are they? v. 22 _____

and v. 25 _____.

What were their problems? _____

and _____. Who was helped

without saying a word? _____

make your Choice

Jesus knows all about me and the problems I face. I can talk to Him anytime, even in my mind through prayer. This is my problem that I need help with today:_____

_____

MONDAY MARK 5:35-43

TAKE THE challenge

check it out!

Are you kidding?

Have you ever been laughed at for something? Jesus was on His way to see Jairus' daughter, when servants from his house came to tell him that his daughter had _____. Jesus explained that Jairus' daughter was not dead, just "_____". What did the people do in v. 40? _____

Unscramble the tiles to find out the most important word Jesus said to Jairus (v. 36b).

e b v e i _____ e l

make your Choice

When I am tempted to give in to fear, whom do I need to turn to?
_____

I will memorize the words in the verse above to help me do this!

TUESDAY MARK 6:1-13

TAKE THE challenge

Where is your faith?

Do you ever feel overlooked in your own home? Jesus, the Son of God, was visiting His hometown and was unable to do many miracles there because of the people's lack of _____. He also sent His disciples out to begin their ministry on the road.

check it out!

Circle what Jesus told His disciples to take with them from vv. 8-10:

pillow　　　**staff**　　　**money**　　　**sandals**　　**cell phone**　　**bread**　　　**bag**　　　**extra coat (tunic)**

make your Choice

How about me? Do I give Jesus room to work in my life by asking and believing by faith when I pray? _____ This is something in my life that I really need to give to God by faith:
_____
_____

WEDNESDAY MARK 6:14-29

check it out!

TAKE THE challenge

A strange request!

Sometimes people do crazy things! Sometimes SIN in a person's life causes him to make poor choices that affect many people. In today's bizarre passage, King Herod put John the Baptist in prison. Let's search out all the facts: Who was angry with John the Baptist (v. 17)? _____

What did King Herod do on his birthday (v. 21)? _____ Who danced for the king and his guests that night (v. 22)? _____

What did Herod offer her (v. 23)? _____

What did she ask for (v.24)? _____

What happened to John in the end (v. 27)? _____

make your Choice

John the Baptist was a great man of God who paid the ultimate price by giving his life for God. He didn't compromise his commitment to the truth, even though it cost him his life! When do I find it hard to stand up for God? _____

_____

THURSDAY MARK 6:30-44

check it out!

TAKE THE challenge

By the numbers!

There are many numbers in today's passage, most of them miraculous when you stop to think about it!   Find the numbers in these verses: How many . . . Loaves of bread _____ v. 38   Fishes _____ v. 38

Baskets of food left over _____ v. 42

Men that ate _____ v. 44

make your Choice

How would I feel if I had been there that day? _____

_____ Like the giving boy in the story, what small thing in my life might Jesus want to take and use to bless many, many people? _____

TAKE THE challenge

check it out!

Is it a ghost?

The disciples are rowing to the other side of the lake when they see something coming toward them! Is it a ghost? No! It's Jesus walking on the water. Draw a picture here of what you think this scene would look like:

make your Choice

Write out the encouraging words that Jesus said to the terrified disciples (v. 50b), and memorize them for a time when you go through a scary time: "_____

_____

_____!"

TAKE THE challenge

check it out!

Wash your hands?

The _____ were upset because the _____ were hungry and were eating without _____their _____. The Pharisees would never do anything except what their religious laws allowed, but they didn't even recognize _____ as the Messiah! They were too busy following "the rules" (that they made up) of their religion! Jesus wants us to show our love for Him by _____ Him. Where do we look to find out how we can obey and live in a way that pleases God? Unscramble the letters to get the answer: **The EBBIL** __ __ __ __ __

make your Choice

What are some ways that I can show my love to Jesus? Circle all that apply: obey my parents — eat macaroni — go to church — catch frogs — read my Bible — pray — watch TV — write a love letter to God — spend all my money on myself — sing songs to God

65

chart your course

"MUTE" *means that you are unable to speak. Often people who are deaf (can't hear) are also mute.*

"REBUKE"

means a sharp, stern disapproval of something.

SUNDAY MARK 7:14-23

TAKE THE challenge

check it out!

Are you clean?

Jesus is telling a parable to His disciples. They had been taught that only certain foods were "clean" to eat. But Jesus transforms their thinking. According to v. 21, where does sin start? Find the answer in the hidden word picture below.

make your Choice

Just as I need a daily shower to stay physically clean, I need a "spiritual" cleaning to keep my **HEART** clean from sin. 1 John 1:9 tells me... "_____"
Confessing my sin to God helps keep my heart clean from sin. What do I need to confess today? _____

MONDAY MARK 7:24-37

TAKE THE challenge

The deaf hear and the mute speak!

check it out!

What did Jesus do for the Gentile woman in v. 29?

_____

What did He do for the man in v. 35? _____

_____

What phrase was used to describe Jesus in v. 37 when others heard about His miracles? "He has done _____ _____ w_____."

make your Choice

Could what was said about Jesus be said about me? _____
Do I try to do my best for God every day? _____
What is one area that I could do better in? (for example: be more truthful, be more kind, be more gentle with my words, etc.)

_____

TUESDAY MARK 8:1-10

TAKE THE challenge

The miraculous meal, part 2!

check it out!

Let's compare miracles! Flip back in your Bible to Mark 6:37-44 and keep a bookmark there; then answer these questions: How many men were fed in today's passage? _____ How many in **Mark 6**? _____ How many loaves and fish in today's passage? _____ loaves _____ fish In Mark 6? _____ loaves _____ fish How many baskets of food were left over in today's passage? _____ In Mark 6? _____ What other things are the same in these two passages? _____

_____

make your Choice

How long had these people been listening to Jesus teach in v. 2?
_____ How hungry would I be after three days with nothing to eat? _____ Who is the only one who can satisfy the deep hunger in my heart? _____ I will praise Jesus right now for saving me and satisfying my "heart hunger"!

67

WEDNESDAY MARK 8:11-26

TAKE THE challenge

check it out!

Check out the signs?

What do these signs tell us to do?

S_____ **Y**_____ **NO** _____

Jesus had already done many miracles to prove who He was, and yet the Pharisees wanted more. Do you think that they truly wanted to believe in Jesus or were they just trying to trick Him? _____

make your ChOjce

What do I think about Jesus? Who is He? _____
_____ What things does
He want to do for me? _____
How can I serve Him today? _____

THURSDAY MARK 8:27-33

TAKE THE challenge

check it out!

Am I two-faced?

Peter is involved in two amazing discussions about Jesus in today's passage. First, Peter is asked who he thinks Jesus is in v. 29. What does he say?

"_____ are (art) the _____".

Next, Jesus is talking about His death in v. 31, and Peter begins to rebuke (see Chart Your Course) Jesus. What does Jesus say to Peter? "Get (thee) b_____ M___ , S_____!"

make your ChOjce

How often am I like Peter, praising Jesus one minute and denying His power the next? Circle ways that I might be denying Jesus' power: NOT READING THE BIBLE - NOT PRAYING - TRYING TO WORK OUT MY OWN PROBLEMS - SPEAKING WITHOUT THINKING - FILLING MY MIND WITH UNWHOLESOME THINGS LIKE BAD TV AND MUSIC

68

FRIDAY MARK 9:1-13

TAKE THE challenge

The Trans-fig-a-what?

check it out!

Today's passage talks about the "transfiguration" of Jesus. What three men went on the mountain with Jesus (v.2)? _____ _____ _____

What happened to Jesus in v. 3? _____

_____

Who appeared with Jesus and talked with Him in v.4? _____

_____

make your Choice

Today's passage tells us that the three men were so frightened by what they saw that they didn't know what to say (v. 6)! Have I ever been that frightened? _____ When? _____ Who helped me when I was afraid? _____ If I know Jesus as my Savior, He's only a prayer away, and He will help me when I ask Him! What do I need His help with this week?_____

SATURDAY MARK 9:14-29

TAKE THE challenge

A tough assignment!

check it out!

The disciples tried to cast out an evil spirit but couldn't do it! Only Jesus was powerful enough to defeat this enemy of darkness. See if you can find eight words from today's passage in the word search.

```
W U Q Q J Z S B B J
Q G N D U P R F E S
J E O B I W L Q L U
S B H R E I X I I S
A D I K V L H F E E
M T T E H D I E V J
R E Y A R P W E E B
M A N S W Q K O F R
L Y W T O G P Q R G
L D Z W B N E J I C
```

**BELIEVE CROWD EVIL JESUS
MAN PRAYER SON SPIRIT UNBELIEF**

make your Choice

Only Jesus is powerful enough to save people from their sin and the power of Satan. Who is someone I am praying for that needs Jesus as his Savior? _____

I will pray for that person right now and EVERY day next week!

chart your course

Will you be indignant this week as you read? I hope not, since indignant means angry, resentful, or mad!

SUNDAY   MARK 9:30-32

TAKE THE challenge

Have you ever been afraid to ask a question?

Jesus was explaining some things to His disciples, but they didn't understand what He was saying and were afraid to ask Him to explain further.

check it out!

In your own words, tell what three things Jesus tried to explain to the disciples in v. 31: _____

_____

_____

make your Choice

Have I understood the truth of the gospel? When and WHERE did I come to know Jesus as my personal Savior? _____

_____

_____

MONDAY MARK 9:33-41

TAKE THE challenge

check it out!

Who's the greatest?

Have you ever been the best at something? Maybe you're the best basketball player at your school, or you've won the spelling bee, or even achieved gold level at Olympians! In verse 35, Jesus tells us who will be the greatest in His kingdom! Unscramble the letters here for the answer: **TVAERSN** __ __ __ __ __ __ __

make your Choice

Look at the word you unscrambled above. Write some words that you think describe a person like that. Here are a couple of words to get you started: HUMBLE - KIND _____

_____

TUESDAY MARK 10:13-16

TAKE THE challenge

Let the kids come!

Jesus loves children! How do you know? Write verse 16 here: "_____

_____

_____ "

According to this verse, Jesus was blessing the boys and girls with affection and tenderness, just like good moms and dads do!

make your Choice

What does it mean to receive Jesus? (circle one) BUY A BIBLE — ASK HIM TO FORGIVE MY SIN AND COME INTO MY HEART — DOWNLOAD CHRISTIAN SONGS ONTO MY IPOD — GO TO CHURCH A LOT. What friend can I share this truth with this week? _____

_____

71

TAKE THE challenge

check it out!

Money, Money, Money!

This is a true story about a rich young man who asked Jesus' advice about how to get into Heaven. Match the following:

____1. "Good Teacher (Master), what must I do to

____2. "No one is good

____3. "You lack one thing:

____4. He went away sad

____5. It's really hard for

A. Because he had great wealth (possessions).

B. Inherit eternal life?"

C. A rich man to enter God's kingdom (be saved).

D. Except God alone."

E. Go sell all you have, give to the poor, and follow ME."

make your Choice

Can my money or "stuff" help me to get to Heaven? _____
What is something that is valuable to me that I might be able to share with someone else? (Such as: Getting my hair cut and giving it to young cancer patients, giving some of my allowance to a missionary, giving a special toy to a child who has none, being a helper to a mom with small children), other: _____

TAKE THE challenge

check it out!

I call shotgun!

Have you ever wanted to sit in the best seat in the car or at a ball game or concert?

What two disciples wanted to sit next to Jesus in Heaven? J __ __ __ __ and J __ __ __ How did this make the other disciples feel (v. 41)?

_____ (See Chart Your Course.)

make your Choice

How do I feel when others win awards and recognition that I feel I should receive? Do I have a good attitude when I win and when I lose a game? *Lord, help me to be happy for others when they are praised above me, and help me to show love whether I win or lose a game, so that people will know that I love YOU. Amen.*

FRIDAY MARK 10:46-52

TAKE THE challenge

check it out!

"What can I do for you?"

BARTIMAEUS STARTS →

What was Bartimaeus doing to try to get Jesus' attention? (v. 47) _____

Help Bartimaeus find his way to Jesus in this maze.

make your Choice

What did Jesus do for this man? Restored his _____
_____ What is something I need
Jesus to help me with? _____
_____ I will pray about this right now!

SATURDAY MARK 11:1-11

TAKE THE challenge

check it out!

A shout of Praise!

What two things were the people laying on the
road? _____ and _____
What were the people shouting?
"_____!" (The exclamation
"hosanna" means "Lord, be gracious and merciful to
us!" What did Jesus ride on? _____

make your Choice

Jesus is the Living Messiah! Just think how amazing it would have been
to be on that road waving branches and praising Jesus! ~ Why not praise
Him right now? Try singing a song of worship to Jesus, and then thank
Him in prayer for Who He is and what He has done for you.

73

chart your course

What will happen in the end times? How will we know when they are coming? Jesus answers these questions in Mark this week!

SUNDAY MARK 11:12-24

TAKE THE challenge

Do you like Fig Newtons? Today we are going to check out a mysterious fig tree!

Fill in the rest of the cartoon strip with what happened in verses 13, 14, and 21

check it out!

make your choice

The disciples were amazed with what happened to the fig tree, but Jesus declared that if they "have faith in God" (v.22), extraordinary things could be accomplished! What is something (that seems impossible) that I need to bring to God in prayer by faith?

MONDAY MARK 11:25-33

TAKE THE challenge

check it out!

"Is that your final answer?"

What question did the chief priests ask Jesus in v. 28? "_____
_____" Jesus answered their question with a question about John the Baptist's teaching. What final answer did they come up with in v. 33? Write it here: "W_____." The chief priests had to either admit that John (and therefore Jesus) was sent from _____, or call him a liar in front of all the people who loved him. So instead, they gave the answer you wrote above.

make your Choice

Sometimes I find it hard to admit to others that I am a Christian. **TRUE / FALSE** I want to speak up for Jesus, but I never know what to say. **TRUE / FALSE** *Lord, please give me the courage to talk about You when others ask me about You, and give me the words to say."* Signed _____

TUESDAY MARK 12:1-12

TAKE THE challenge

check it out!

Will they respect My Son?

Find the words from today's parable in the puzzle.

```
U P Y N Y S T X H P
S C J X L S L V A D
F E K C O E I I R N
V X R N T R F A V F
U I O V D P Y H E A
J S T B A E N W S L
T R A O N N L F T L
Z H I I O I T L L A
O T V X Q W T G I W
B E A T I N G S H K
```

**BEATINGS   HARVEST   KILLED
SERVANT   SON
VINEYARD   WALL**

make your Choice

Do I respect Jesus as the Son of God? Do I obey my parents and listen to them?... Listen attentively to the Word of God?...Show respect for adults by not talking back? - I will underline one of these that I need to work on this week.

WEDNESDAY MARK 12:13-17

TAKE THE challenge

check it out!

Do we have to pay taxes?

Again the Pharisees were trying to trick Jesus with their questions. How did Jesus answer their question about taxes? He asked for a _____ in v. 15. Whose picture was on it _____ (v.16)? Jesus' answer is found in v. 17: "_____ to Caesar _____ and _____ God_____."

make your Choice

Am I faithful in honoring God with my money? _____
What is something I can do to earn money to give to God this week? _____
_____

THURSDAY MARK 12:41-44

TAKE THE challenge

check it out!

She gave the most!

In one of the money sacks, draw how much money the rich people were putting into the temple offering. Now, in the other sack, draw how much money the widow put into the temple offering.

Whom did Jesus say put in more? _____
WHY? _____

make your Choice

Am I giving Jesus my all? Do I put my time with Him first before everything else? _____ Do I give what I can to Jesus from my money? _____ Do I offer to help others (without being asked) as my service to Jesus? YES / NO

76

FRIDAY MARK 13:1-13

TAKE THE challenge

check it out!

How will we know when these things will happen?

Jesus is speaking to His disciples about the end times. What are some things He says will happen in these times? (Unscramble the following words.)

RWAS __ __ __ __

EFAINMS __ __ __ __ __ __ __

QRETAHKSEAU __ __ __ __ __ __ __ __ __ __ __

make your Choice

Jesus is coming back for me someday, IF I know Him as my Savior from sin. Am I ready for His return? _____ What would I want Jesus to find me doing if He were to come back today?

_____

_____

SATURDAY MARK 13:14-23

TAKE THE challenge

check it out!

Is it Jesus?

Jesus tells the disciples that in the last days many will come claiming to be Him. What is His command to them (at the end of v. 21) when they heard these untrue things?

" _____

_____ "

make your Choice

What do I do when I hear something about Jesus or the Bible that I think might not be true? Circle all you should do: ASK MY PARENTS -- ASK A YOUTH LEADER — READ THE BIBLE MYSELF — DO SOME RESEARCH ONLINE — ASK MY PASTOR — PRAY FOR RIGHT ANSWERS. 77

chart your course

NARD - *a very costly perfume*

ANOINT - *to pour on*

ALABASTER - *smooth and white; often a smooth type of stone much like marble.*

SUNDAY MARK13:24-37

TAKE THE challenge

One thing never changes!

check it out!

In verse 31, Jesus makes an important statement. See if you can crack the code to find out what this statement is: "Heaven and earth will pass away, but

_ _   _ _ _ _ _   _ _ _   _ _ _ _ _   _ _ _ _   _ _ _ _."
6 14   13 8 10 2 11   13 4 5 5   7 3 12 3 10   9 1 11 11   1 13 1 14

CODE: 1=A 2=D 3=E 4=I 5=L 6=M 7=N 8=O 9=P 10=R 11=S 12=V 13=W 14=Y

make your Choice

Jesus promises that His Word will stand forever! How much importance do I place on getting God's Word into my life? (Circle one.) God's Word is: very important   somewhat important   important sort of important   not important at all   in my life. How do I prove this? _____

MONDAY MARK14:1-11

A beautiful act and a betraying antagonist!

check it out!

Jesus is at the home of a man named Simon when something is done to Him which no one expects. What did a woman do to Jesus at the end of v. 3?

_____

This seems strange to us, but to Jesus, it was a beautiful act of love and worship. (See Chart Your Course.) Who is mentioned in v. 10? _____ To whom was He speaking? _____ Why? _____ What would He receive for this act? _____

make your Choice

If I know Jesus as my Savior, at times I am like both of these people. Sometimes I do things that please Jesus, and sometimes I fall into sin. What should I do when I sin? _____ _____ What will Jesus do for me if I ask Him? _____

TUESDAY MARK14:12-21

TAKE THE challenge

"Is it me, Lord?"

check it out!

In v. 18, Jesus states that one of the disciples was going to betray Him. Today, we know who that was; but then, the disciples really didn't know who would betray Jesus. Each one of them asked, "Is it I, Lord?" Do a little research! Look up John 13:2 to see who this betrayer was. Now unscramble his name:

SAUJD CRIOAIST _ _ _ _ _   _ _ _ _ _ _ _ _

make your Choice

If I know Jesus, I can betray His holiness by my sin. BUT He promises forgiveness for my sin if I ask for it. What sin do I need to ask forgiveness for right now? _____

Jesus, I thank You so much for Your forgiveness and grace, even when I turn my back on You sometimes.

79

TAKE THE challenge

Does your church have "communion services" each month or week?

check it out!

Communion at church is a time when we remember what Jesus did for us by dying on the cross. The first communion actually took place before Jesus died, when He was with His disciples here in this passage. Look at today's verses. What does the bread represent? _____

What does the wine represent? _____

Why do we have communion according to Jesus? 1 Corinthians 11:25b

Do this _____ r_____ of _____.

make your Choice

Do I participate in communion? _____ Am I thankful to Jesus for what He did for me on the cross? _____

Do I show this by paying attention, thinking about Jesus' death for me, and listening during communion? _____

TAKE THE challenge

Are you still sleeping?

check it out!

What is Jesus doing in these verses? (v. 32)

RAYPNGI __ __ __ __ __ __ __

(Unscramble the answer.) [If JESUS needed to pray, surely we all need to be praying more, huh?]

What are the disciples doing in these verses? (v. 41)

EEINSLPG __ __ __ __ __ __ __ __

What could the disciples have done to help Jesus and show their support to Him? _____

_____

make your Choice

When I have a friend who needs my help, what is the most important thing I can do for that person? _____

What else might I do to help? _____

FRIDAY MARK 14:43-52

Watch for the signal!

check it out!

Unscramble the four words from today's passage, then write the secret word in the final box from the circled letters above.

DANEK (v. 52) ___ ___ ( ) ___ ___

PURECRISST (v. 49B)
___ ___ ___ ( ) ___ ___ ___ ___ ___ ___

SADJU (vv. 43,45) ___ ___ ___ ___ ( )

SJESU (vv. 45,48,51) ___ ___ ( ) ___ ___

Secret word: ___ ___ ___ ___

make your Choice

What would I have done if I was with Jesus when this happened? One disciple (Peter) drew his _____ to defend Jesus and cut off a guard's _____! Another turned and _____ away naked! What do I do when someone asks me about Jesus?

_____

_____

SATURDAY MARK 14:53-65

The sixty-four million dollar question: "Are you the Christ?"

check it out!

What a terrible scene! People are lying to the chief priests about Jesus and making up stories about Him. What does Jesus do in the midst of all of this in verse 61?

_____

At long last, they ask Him if He is the Christ. How does Jesus answer them (v. 62)? _____

What happens to Jesus after this in verse 65? _____

_____

make your Choice

Whom do I say that Jesus is? _____

_____ I will take time right now to praise Him for everything He is and everything He does for me. He is my Messiah and the ONLY ONE Who can save me!

81

chart your course

Just IMAGINE... huge thorns in your head... beatings... scourgings (cruel whippings with rocks and glass shards woven into the nine cords of the whip)... and people making fun of you!?!? This is awful! - Yet, this is what our Savior, Jesus, endured for each of us... Read about it and be thankful this week!

SUNDAY MARK 14:66-72

TAKE THE Challenge

A strange kind of alarm clock!

Back in Mark 14:30-31, Peter makes quite a statement! He claims that he will never _____ Jesus. Jesus, however, knows Peter's heart. Write Peter's "denial statements" below:

PETER'S DENIAL STATEMENTS In v. 68 he says:
" _____
_____." In v. 70 he denies that he knows Jesus again.
In v. 71 he says: " _____
_____."What did Peter do at the end of v. 72? _____ Why? _____

check it out!

make your Choice

Was there ever a time when I caused others to think I wasn't a Christian by the way I talked or acted? _____ How did I feel afterwards?_____
Is there a time when I spoke up about Jesus? _____
How did I feel afterwards? _____

MONDAY MARK 15:1-15

check it out!

Don't do it!

Pilate does something in v. 15 that we all do at times. It says, "willing to content the crowd" (KJV) or "wishing to satisfy the crowd" (NASB). Put a check mark by some of these things kids might do to satisfy their crowd of friends. SMOKE **TAKE DRUGS** ACT OUT IN CLASS USE CRUDE LANGUAGE MAKE FUN OF OTHERS LEAVE SOMEONE OUT OF A GAME WATCH A BAD MOVIE DRINK ALCOHOL **STEAL SOMETHING** TELL A LIE (OR EXAGGERATE THE TRUTH) LAUGH AT ANOTHER'S EXPENSE OTHER_____

make your Choice

What things have I done to impress or please my friends? (circle them above) Would these things please Jesus? _____ How could I act differently next time?_____ _____ _____

TUESDAY MARK 15:16-26

check it out!

Would you carry Jesus' cross?

In v. 21, the Bible tells us who carries Jesus' cross when He is too weak (from all His beatings) to carry it Himself. Write his name here: _____ What were his son's names? A _____ and R_____. This family had made the journey to the Passover celebration from Cyrene, a colony in North Africa.

make your Choice

What a privilege it would be to carry the cross for the Savior! I can "carry the cross" of Jesus when I choose to be obedient and faithful even in the midst of hard times. Something that is hard for me right now is: _____. I will pray right now about how I can "carry this cross" for Jesus.

WEDNESDAY MARK 15:27-38

TAKE THE challenge

check it out!

On the day that Jesus died.

Many things happened on the day Jesus died. Complete the word search to find out some of the things that happened.

S	S	E	N	K	R	A	D	N	T
N	X	V	X	S	I	C	G	I	O
U	E	A	O	R	J	N	K	A	R
E	R	K	O	I	I	P	O	T	N
Q	H	U	A	K	C	L	E	R	S
S	T	O	C	S	O	E	V	U	N
X	R	O	D	U	R	A	O	C	O
H	M	R	D	R	K	O	J	S	R
I	N	S	U	L	T	S	F	Z	X
I	Q	G	B	M	Q	Z	D	U	J

CURTAIN   DARKNESS
FORSAKEN   INSULTS   LOUD
MOCKING   TORN   VOICE

make your Choice

I should praise Jesus for the gift of salvation that He provided for me by dying in my place for my sin. I will write my prayer of thanksgiving here: *Dear Jesus,* _____
_____

Love, _____

THURSDAY MARK 15:39-47

TAKE THE challenge

check it out!

Who was this man?

After everything that had happened, many people still didn't believe in Jesus. However, the guard that stood next to the cross did! What did he say in v. 39 about who Jesus was? "_____
_____!" After Jesus died, a man came to get Jesus to bury Him. What do we know about this man? Name? _____

Occupation?_____ What was he waiting for?_____ Whom did he ask if he could bury Jesus? _____

make your Choice

Do I believe that Jesus is the Son of God, the Messiah? _____
Is there one of my friends that doesn't know this truth?_____
_____ Lord Jesus, I pray for _____
that he will come to know You and the truth of Your death on the cross for him. Amen.

84

FRIDAY MARK 16:1-8

TAKE THE challenge

check it out!

Where did He go?

What were the women going to do when they got to the tomb? _____

What were they worried about? _____
_____

What did they find when they got there? _____
_____

Who spoke to them and sat on the stone? _____

What did he tell them? "_____!"

make your Choice

Can I imagine what it would be like to be grieving over someone I loved who was dead, only to be told that He was alive! How amazing! I will write what I would be feeling if I were these women: _____
_____ Now thank Jesus for being a LIVING Savior!

SATURDAY MARK 16:9-20

TAKE THE challenge

check it out!

Get ready! Get set! Now GO!

Jesus appeared to many people after He rose from the dead. Who was the first person He appeared to? _____ What did she do as soon as she saw Jesus alive? _____
_____
_____ When He met with His disciples later, He gave them (and all Christians to this day) this very important command: "Go _____
_____."

make your Choice

How can I live out this command of Jesus today, this week, my whole life? _____
Maybe I should start praying that God will help me to become a missionary and take His gospel message to people in another part of the world someday!

85

chart your course

FORMER FISHERMAN TURNED AUTHOR!!

John was probably a cousin of Jesus and had been a fisherman before he followed Jesus. He became one of Jesus' three best friends! His name means Jehovah is given. John wrote five entire books of the Bible. Guess which ones! (answers at bottom of page)

SUNDAY 1 JOHN 1:1-4

TAKE THE challenge

Have you ever been an eyewitness to an accident or a special event?

check it out!

Take a moment to look back at this author's FIRST book: John 1:1. In both books, he describes Jesus as the _____ sent from heaven to earth. John claims to be a witness to Jesus' being on earth as a man. He says he had _____ upon Him or at Him, and had even _____Him with his hands. What was the main reason John was writing this letter? "So that our (circle one) **JOY ~ SORROW ~ PEACE** would be full or complete!"

make your Choice

How can I witness to someone today about what Christ has done in my life? _____
_____

Chart Your Course Answer: John, I John, II John, III John, Revelation

MONDAY 1 JOHN 1:5-10

TAKE THE challenge

Be honest! Are you ever afraid of the dark?

check it out!

Here's the big MESSAGE: God is _____; and in

Him is no _____ at _____. If we _____

in the _____ as He is in the _____

we have _____ with each other and the _____

of Jesus . . . . _____ us from all _____.

make your Choice

Will I choose to walk in Christ's light or sin's darkness? _____
_____

How can I "walk in His light" today? _____
_____

TUESDAY 1 JOHN 2:1-6

TAKE THE challenge

Know any lawyers? You might need one someday!

check it out!

John says he writes this letter so that we won't

___ ___ ___. BUT, if (when) we do sin, we have the

best lawyer (one who speaks to the Father in our

defense – an advocate) in the universe to plead our

sinful case before God: " _____ _____, the

_____ " (One).

make your Choice

Verse 4 reminds me that if I truly KNOW Christ, I'll _____
His _____." In verse 6, if I say I live (abide) in Christ,
I will _____ just like my Savior, Jesus!
How am I doing?

WEDNESDAY 1 JOHN 2:7-11

check it out!

Have you ever caught yourself saying, "I HATE you!" to someone in anger?

Look back at John 13:34 to see what "new commandment" he is referring to in verses 7-8. Finish the chart below:

LIGHT

v. 7 - _____ commandment

v. 10 a - _____ his brother

v. 10b – Nothing to cause him to _____ because he's _____

DARKNESS

v. 7 - _____ commandment

v. 9 - _____ his brother

v. 11 — Doesn't know where he is

make your Choice

Am I walking in the light of Christ's love or the darkness of hatred and bitterness? _____ Whom do I need to make things right with today? _____
_____

THURSDAY 1 JOHN 2:12-17

check it out!

Do you ever wonder what God's will is for you?

Match the following from the passage:

_____ 1. Sins forgiven, has known the Father

_____ 2. Known Him Who's from the beginning

_____ 3. Overcome the evil one; strong

_____ 4. DO NOT

_____ 5. Lives forever

A. Whoever does God's will

B. Young men

C. Love the world

D. Children

E. Fathers

make your Choice

What can I be doing each day to help me find, know, and do God's will? _____
_____

FRIDAY 1 JOHN 2:18-22

TAKE THE challenge

check it out!

Can anyone be an antichrist?

John tells his "children" in the faith that this is the

_____, in verse 18, and that _____

will be coming. Then he says in verse 22 the TRUTH

is that antichrist = One who _____

the _____ and the _____.

An _____ is a liar!

make your Choice

Do I read and study my Bible enough to know if I were to meet an

antichrist? _____ Anyone who is "anti"

or "against" trusting Jesus is _____.

SATURDAY 1 JOHN 2:23-27

TAKE THE challenge

check it out!

How do you know God's Holy Spirit is living inside you?

Again – let's look back to John's gospel and do a

little detective work to see who he's referring to

here as "the anointing" we've received of (from)

God. Look up John 15:26. Jesus is talking about

sending the _____ who is the

_____ of _____ to be with them and help them.

1 John 2:27 reminds us that this "anointing" " _____ in you"

and _____ us all things.

make your Choice

God's Holy Spirit lives in _____ and teaches me from

God's _____ each day as I have my Quiet Time.

chart your course

The Apostle John was a prolific author. (That means he wrote a bunch of books!) He not only wrote the three letters of 1, 2, and 3 John, but the Gospel of John and The Revelation. He wrote Revelation from the small, wild island of Patmos where he'd been exiled for his faith.

SUNDAY 1 JOHN 2:28-3:3

TAKE THE challenge

How prepared are you for Christ's coming? What if He was coming back in just one hour?

check it out!

Did you notice all the references to Christ's Second Coming as you read this passage? Circle them below:

"WHEN HE APPEARS" **"DEAR CHILDREN"**

"THIS HOPE" **"HE IS RIGHTEOUS"**

"WHEN HE APPEARS" **"WE SHALL SEE HIM"**

Verse 3 says that everyone who has this _____ in Him

_____ himself, even (just) as HE is _____.

make your Choice

What do I need to let God change or purify in my life so I'm ready

for Jesus' coming? _____

_____

MONDAY 1 JOHN 3:4-10

check it out!

Do people ever compare me to one of my parents and say I look like them?

Complete the chart:

CHILDREN OF GOD

v. 6a – Stop

_____

v. 7b – Does

_____

v. 9b – God's

s_____ remaineth

CHILDREN OF THE DEVIL

v. 6b – Continue to

_____

v. 10b – Does (doeth) not

_____

v. 10c – Does not love his

_____

(remains) in him

make your Choice

Which side do I fit into? - Am I acting more like Satan's child than God's child? YES / NO   What do I need to let God change in my life?

_____

_____

TUESDAY 1 JOHN 3:11-16

check it out!

How would you know a murderer if you met one?

Who murdered his brother out of jealousy?

_____ What should we not be surprised at or marvel about? "If the _____

_____ you (v. 13). " What's one of the biggest evidences that someone has passed from

death into life? "We _____ the (our) _____."

How is a MURDERER identified in verse 15? Someone who

_____ his _____!

make your Choice

Have I ever murdered someone in my heart by hating them?

_____

Whose example of sacrificial love do I need to follow (v. 16)?

_____

91

WEDNESDAY 1 JOHN 3:17-24

check it out!

Has anyone ever told you they cared about you and then done nothing to prove it?

Let's do a counting game today! Look back over all of chapter 3. How many times do you count the word "love" or any form of that word? ⬜
Now count the word "brother". ("brethren" in the King James version). ⬜ That's a lot of times, huh? Verse 18 reminds us that true love is NOT just loving in (with) _____ or _____, but with (in) _____ and in _____.

make your Choice

How do I best prove or show my love for someone else? _____

_____

_____

THURSDAY 1 JOHN 4:1-6

check it out!

How do you know who to believe or trust in today's world?

Complete the contrasting chart below:

SPIRIT OF GOD	SPIRIT OF ANTICHRIST
v. 1 – From _____	**v. 1** – Not from _____
	v. 1 - _____ prophets
v. 2 – Confesses or acknowledges that _____ has come in the _____.	**v. 3** – Does not acknowledge or confess _____
	v. 3b – Already in the _____
v. 6a - _____ to believers	
v. 6c – Spirit of _____	**v. 6b** – Does not _____ to believers
	v. 6c – Spirit of _____

make your Choice

I can claim God's wonderful promise in verse 4:
I can _____ false spirits because the Spirit of Christ in me is _____ than the one in the _____ ! Am I living like it? YES / NO

FRIDAY 1 JOHN 4:7-12

TAKE THE Challenge

check it out!

How would you define "love"?

How many times is the word "love" used in these 6 verses? ⬜ How did God manifest (show or prove) His love for us (v. 9)? _____

_____

_____

The definition of "love" is in verse 10: "Herein (this) is love, NOT that we loved _____, but that _____ loved us and _____ His _____ to be the _____ for our sins."

make your Choice

Whom can I tell about Jesus' love this week? _____

_____

SATURDAY 1 JOHN 4:13-21

TAKE THE Challenge

What are you most afraid of?

check it out!

Verse 16 tells us that G_____ = I_____.

Whoever _____ in love _____

in _____, and _____ lives in him!

What cannot co-exist with love? _____

According to verse 19, why do we love? Because

_____ first _____ _____.

make your Choice

What am I most afraid of? _____

How can God's love take away my fear? _____

_____

_____

chart your course

How can someone know for sure that he is a Christian? - One of God's own children? - Born again? John gives all the "birthmarks" of a true believer in these books. Check off those which are true of you!

- [ ] **Regular fellowship with Christ and other Christians**
- [ ] **Confessed sins** [ ] **Loves others**
- [ ] **God's Spirit indwells him** [ ] **Obeys God's commands**
- [ ] **Loves God, not the world** [ ] **Has prayers answered**
- [ ] **Does not continue in sin**

SUNDAY 1 JOHN 5:1-8

TAKE THE challenge

Have you ever won a contest or a game? How does victory feel?

check it out!

Verse 3 tells us that true love for God is shown by

_____ His _____. Who overcomes the

world (v. 4)? _____

_____ Our faith is the _____ that

_____ the world! What's the right answer

to "Who is he that overcomes the world?" He who

believes _____ is the _____ of _____.

make your Choice

How will I be victorious over this evil world in which I live? _____

_____

_____

MONDAY 1 JOHN 5:9-15

How confident are you that God really answers prayer?

How many times do you count the word "life" in this passage? ☐   Match the following:

check it out!

_____ 1. Whoever has the Son

_____ 2. Does NOT have life

_____ 3. You may KNOW

_____ 4. He hears us pray

A. That you have eternal life

B. Has life

C. The confidence we have in God

D. Whoever does NOT have the Son of God

make your Choice

If I really believe God answers prayer, what will I be doing every

day? _____

_____

TUESDAY 1 JOHN 5:16-21

When you hear about an "idol," what do you picture?

Verse 18 tells us that anyone (whosoever) born of God does not what? Who do you think "the wicked one" ("evil one") in verse 18 is? _____

check it out!

(HINT: 1 John 3:12) What is the last thing the Apostle John tells his young believers here? "_____

_____ "

make your Choice

What is one thing that is or could become an idol (anything that gets more of my attention than God) in my life? _____

_____

_____

WEDNESDAY 2 JOHN 1-6

check it out!

How would you want others to describe you?

To whom does John write this little letter? "the

_____ _____ and her

_____" This "lady" could have either

been a person or a church (group of believers).

What were two things that were true of the

"children" here? (Circle them.) JOHN LOVED THEM IN TRUTH.

THEY HAD BEEN VERY DISOBEDIENT. THEY WERE WALKING IN THE TRUTH.

make your Choice

If my pastor or church leader were to describe me, would he say that I am "walking in the truth"? YES / NO   Why or why not?

_____

_____

THURSDAY 2 JOHN 7-13

TAKE THE challenge

check it out!

Is there a friend or relative you write or send e-mail messages to regularly?

Complete the crossword puzzle:

1-Won't write with _____ and ink (v. 12)

2-He has both the _____ and the Son (v. 9)

3-An _____ is one who doesn't confess Jesus Christ in the flesh (v. 7).

4-Hope (trust) to come to you _____ to face. (v. 12)

5-Don't receive a deceiver into your _____. (v. 10)

6-Be careful not to _____ what you've worked for (wrought). (v. 8)

make your Choice

Circle deceivers I should not invite into my home: Baptists, Jehovah's Witnesses, My pastor, Muslims, New Age people, Mormons, Satan worshipers, Buddhists

FRIDAY 3 JOHN 1-8

check it out!

Has anyone bragged on you lately?

John brags on his friend, _____ and prays for him here. Put a "B" beside the BRAGS and a "P" by the PRAYER requests below.

_____ That you may prosper and be in good health.

_____ Your soul prospers (does well).

_____ You continue to walk in the truth.

_____ You are faithful to help your brothers as well as strangers.

_____ You have love (charity).

make your Choice

Which thing above would I like someone to see in my life? (Check it.)

SATURDAY 3 JOHN 9-14

TAKE THE challenge

Can you think of a friend who's a good influence on you and one who's a bad influence?

check it out!

John compares two men here: _____ and _____ Draw a line from each of these young men to the things that describe them.

DEMETRIUS

DIOTREPHES

Loves being # 1
Gossiping with malicious words
Well spoken of (good report) by everyone truthful
Refuses to receive (welcome) the brothers at church
Is good and from God

make your Choice

Who are my best friends? _____

_____ Which of them is truly a good influence on my life? _____

Israel had been in captivity in Babylon for 70 years because of their sin. Ezra was one of the captives, and he was:

1. **A PRIEST** *(someone who talked to God on behalf of the people)*

2. **A SCRIBE** *(someone who studied, copied, and taught the scriptures)*

Ezra tells the exciting story of the rebuilding of the temple (house of worship) in Jerusalem.

SUNDAY EZRA 1:1-11

Did you know that God always uses PEOPLE to accomplish His work?

Who was the King of Persia? _____ Where did God tell him to build His temple (His house of worship)? _____ Cyrus allowed anyone to go up to Jerusalem (v.3). He even said, "_____ be with him." Did every Israelite go to build God's house? _____ What did those who stayed behind do to help and encourage those who went? _____

Go? Or Give? God wants me to go to _____ to do His work. God wants me to give _____ to help with His work.

MONDAY EZRA 2:1, 64-70

TAKE THE challenge

check it out!

How much should I give?

How many people traveled to Judah? (Remember, "score" stands for 20.)

People   __ __ , 3 6 0

Servants   7 , __ __ __

+ Singers   __ __ __ __
_____

TOTAL

Verse 69 tells how they gave: "according to their _____".

make your Choice

How much do I spend on: Snacks_____ Clothes_____
Jewlery_____ Music_____ Games_____ ?
If I spend this much on myself, how much should I be giving to God?

TUESDAY EZRA 3:1-13

TAKE THE challenge

check it out!

Why is the cross such a special symbol to believers?

What was the first thing that the people rebuilt?
_____What did they do then?
_____

These "sacrifices" were animals offered on the altar to cover the sins of the people. To us, the cross is our altar. Who was our sacrifice on the cross? _____

make your Choice

Thank you, _____, for dying on the cross as a sacrifice for my sins! I HAVE / HAVE NOT (circle one) accepted Your only sacrifice for my sins.

TAKE THE challenge

check it out!

What causes you to feel discouraged?

Circle the correct choice for each question. Who offered help with the building project? **FRIENDS / ADVERSARIES (ENEMIES)** (v.5) Their enemies hired c_____ to frustrate their _____. Did the leaders allow them to help? **YES / NO**

make your Choice

When people try to discourage me from doing God's will, I need to _____.

TAKE THE challenge

check it out!

A letter to the King! Can you always believe what you read?

Which city did the letter describe as wicked and rebellious? _____ The letter also predicted that the people would not pay their _____. But how could these accusations be true? _____ was God's city!

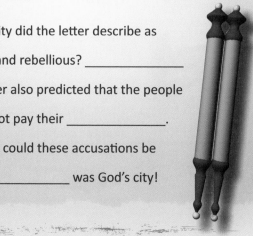

make your Choice

When I read something, I will make sure it is true before I _____.

100

FRIDAY EZRA 4:17-24

TAKE THE challenge

check it out!

Can a letter from the king stop God's work?

In the letter, the king gave the order to _____

the work of building the _____.

But . . . the work stopped only until the second

year of the reign of King _____.

make your ChOjce

Help me to remember that _____ is in control

and men cannot do anything to stop His work forever.

SATURDAY EZRA 5:1-5

TAKE THE challenge

check it out!

Remember that someone is always watching!

Two _____ preached to the people about

building the _____ of God. Unscramble

their names here: **GAHAIG** __ __ __ __ __ __

CHARZIHAE __ __ __ __ __ __ __ __ __ (Can

you find their prophecies in your Bible?) Did

someone harass them as they worked? _____

What was watching over them as they worked? "The _____

_____ _____ _____ "

make your ChOjce

Knowing that God is watching should make me feel _____

when I'm doing good and _____ when I'm sinning.

chart your course

IMAGINE... if you were one of the Israelites returning from Babylon to Jerusalem.

FIRST... Remember that you've never been there. (The captivity probably started before you were born!)

SECOND... The trip took at least 4 months

THIRD... You traveled mostly on foot, or by donkey or camel, because there were no airplanes, buses, trains, or cars.

SUNDAY EZRA 5:6-17

TAKE THE challenge

What TITLE would you like to have? Doctor? President? Executive Director? Professor?

check it out!

In today's passage, find the title that God's people who were rebuilding the temple gave themselves.

"We are the _____ of the _____ of h_____ and e_____" (v. 11)

Wow! What more impressive title could you have? What do you have to do to be a servant? Simply __b __y!

make your Choice

I want to be a servant of God. Today, I will _____

_____

_____ to show my obedience to Him.

TAKE THE challenge

A search for proof!

check it out!

DOWN
1. Where were they to rebuild?
5. Who did Ezra want them to pray for? The king and his _____ (v. 10)

ACROSS
2. What were they to re-build (v. 3)?
3. Which king wrote the original decree to rebuild?
4. Which king ordered a search for the temple treasures and records?
6. What did the king want them to offer? S_____ (v. 10)

make your Choice

Even people who don't know the Lord want God's people to pray for them. What unbeliever can I pray for today?

_____

TAKE THE challenge

Finally Finished! How do you celebrate a job well-done?

check it out!

WHAT did they celebrate? (v.16)

Kept (celebrated) the d_____ of t_____ h_____ of _____.

HOW did they celebrate? (v.16)

With J_____

WHAT TWO FEASTS did they celebrate?

_____ and _____ of _____

_____

make your Choice

When I celebrate, I will always give _____ praise, because everything worth celebrating comes from Him! Today I am celebrating and thanking God for_____

WEDNESDAY EZRA 7:1-10

What are some things that are very important to you?

Today's passage tells us that God was gracious to Ezra because he had devoted himself to:

- ☐ Getting Rich
- ☐ Being well-known
- ☐ Having a lot of friends
- ☐ Learning the Word of God
- ☐ Obeying the Word of God
- ☐ Teaching the Word of God

make your Choice

What's more important to me than the Word of God? _____

What keeps me from having my Quiet Time every day?

_____

What excuse do I give for not memorizing Scripture? _____

_____

THURSDAY EZRA 7:11-28

TAKE THE challenge

check it out!

How do you honor the Lord?

Write the verse number from today's passage that tells about each action King Artaxerxes took to honor the Lord

____ Allowed the Israelites to return to Jerusalem

____ Sent money to provide for the financial needs of the temple

____ Did not allow the priests, Levites or other temple servants to be taxed

____ Authorized punishment for those who disobeyed the law of God

make your Choice

Today, I will honor God by _____

_____

FRIDAY EZRA 8:1, 15-23

TAKE THE challenge

check it out!

Do you REALLY trust God, or do you just SAY you trust Him?

Fill in the blanks using the words below to tell how Ezra prepared for the journey. Ezra _____ for a safe journey. Because he had told the king that GOD would _____ them, he was _____ to ask for SOLDIERS to protect them. God _____ their prayer!

Word choices: ANSWERED   ASHAMED   PROTECT   PRAYED

make your Choice

When I pray about something, I . . .
a.   Still worry about it
b.   Try to work it out on my own
c.   Trust God to do what is best

SATURDAY EZRA 8:24-36

TAKE THE challenge

check it out!

Does your Mom or Dad ever say, "You need to be responsible"?

What words in verse 29 tell us that the 12 priests were responsible for the treasures that they were taking to Jerusalem? _____ _____. When did they weigh the treasures? Before the trip s_____ and w_____ they arrived at the temple. This is called accountability, or "proving that they were responsible."

make your Choice

I am willing to be accountable by:
_____ Having Mom or Dad check to be sure my chores are done well.
_____ Having an adult check my Quiet Time each week.
_____ Quoting a verse to my leader, teacher or friend each week.
_____ Having Mom or Dad see everything that I watch on T.V. or the computer.

chart your course

Haggai (say it HAG-AY-EYE) was a prophet of God, and he was pretty fired up because the people were not doing what they had come back to Jerusalem to do - BUILD THE TEMPLE! For years they had not had a place to meet together to worship like God had commanded them.

Prophecy of Haggai

SUNDAY EZRA 9:1-5

TAKE THE challenge

What is your reaction to sin? Does it bother you? Offend you?

check it out!

Carefully search the first two verses and write the words that you find that mean **SIN:**

Verse 1_____ Verse 2_____

Verse 3 describes Ezra's reaction when he heard about the people's sin. What did he do?_____

_____

How did he feel? _____

make your choice

A T.V. show or commercial that tries to get me to laugh at sin is _____. The next time I am with someone who thinks it's funny to do something wrong without getting caught, I will _____.

TAKE THE challenge

Does it matter what kind of friends we choose?

check it out!

Ezra's prayer tells us what sin he was mourning over. What kind of people lived in the land? (v. 11)

_____

Were the Israelites to seek close friendships or marriage with these wicked people? (v. 12)

_____

make your Choice

Before I become a close friend with someone I will find out: (check all that apply

- [ ] If they love God.
- [ ] If they have sinful habits.
- [ ] If they laugh at sin.

TUESDAY EZRA 10:1-9

TAKE THE challenge

When you know you are wrong, what is the right thing to do?

check it out!

"Confess" means to admit what you have done and say it is sin. What did Schecaniah say in verse 2 to show he was confessing their sin? "_____

_____

_____"

"Repent" means that you change your mind and actions to make things right. In verse 3, what action showed repentance? _____

_____

make your Choice

Lord, search my heart and show me my sin. I have sinned by

_____

Help me to _____

_____ to make this right.

107

WEDNESDAY EZRA 10:10-19, 44

TAKE THE challenge

Is it easy to make things right after you have sinned?

check it out!

What did Israel do since they had sinned by

marrying women who were not believers? _____

_____

_____

Do you think this was easy?_____

make your Choice

I want to do the _____ thing even

when it's hard. A friend I may have to give up because he or she

doesn't want to obey God is _____.

THURSDAY HAGGAI 1:1-15

TAKE THE challenge

What is important to you? (Hint: It's whatever you spend your time and money on!)

check it out!

Well, FIFTEEN YEARS after the people returned to
Judah, Haggai the prophet started speaking. What
were the people saying about rebuilding God's house
(v. 2)? "_____

_____" What
had the people been doing while waiting for the
"right time" to begin building? (v. 9) They were busy building _____

_____ The Lord repeated the same

phrase twice (vv. 5, 7). What did he say? "_____

_____"

make your Choice

I have been too busy with _____

_____ to do what I know God wants me to

do. *Lord, help me make time in my life for what You want me to do.*

FRIDAY HAGGAI 2:1-9

TAKE THE
challenge

check it out!

A dirty car, an overgrown garden, dirty dishes, overflowing trash cans... what does it take to make them look good again?

The people remembered what God's _____ used to look like and could see how badly it looked now. God reminded them that to restore the temple, it would take hard _____. What did God promise to give them in their rebuilt temple (v.9)? Find it in the hidden picture below and write it out _____

The opposite of hard-working is _____.

What am I neglecting by being lazy? _____

_____

make your
Choice

Lord, help me to get up and "JUST DO IT!"

SATURDAY HAGGAI 2:10-23

TAKE THE
challenge

check it out!

When you start obeying, Pay Attention! God will bless!

Haggai describes how touching holy things cannot make someone holy, but touching defiled things does make someone defiled (getting next to a sick, germy person will probably make YOU sick!). He also mentions how poor and needy the disobedient people had become. Check out God's promise to the obedient ones at the end of verse 19: "_____

_____ "

make your
Choice

I have been disobeying God by _____

_____. I want to change right now and be obedient to Him from now on.

chart your course

Remember Ezra, the priest, who returned to Jerusalem to rebuild the temple? Well, about fifteen years later, Nehemiah returned to Jerusalem to rebuild the wall around the city. Nehemiah, though Jewish, was a trusted member of the Persian King's court. His job was to test all of the King's food before it was served to make sure it was safe to eat. He was a taste-tester!

SUNDAY NEHEMIAH 1:1-11

TAKE THE challenge

What do you do when you get bad news?

check it out!

Check out the bad news Nehemiah received from Judah in verse 3. What did the report say? "_____
_____
_____ "

What was Nehemiah's reaction to the news? (v. 4) Circle the

things he did: **Laughed**   **Cried**   **Danced**

Fasted   **Watched TV**   **Prayed**   **Slept**   **Ate**

make your Choice

The next time something really upsets me, I will be sure to

remember to p_____ like Nehemiah did.

MONDAY NEHEMIAH 2:1-8

TAKE THE challenge

Have you ever been scared to death when you were talking to someone important?

check it out!

Verse 2 tells us how Nehemiah felt when he went to talk to the king: _____ and _____ What did he do even while he was talking to the king? (v. 4)"_____"

Why did the King grant his request? (v. 8b)_____

_____

make your Choice

I want to remember that I can _____ to God _____ time and _____ place.

TUESDAY NEHEMIAH 2:9-20

TAKE THE challenge

When you are excited about a project, is it always easy to get started?

check it out!

Pick the answers for the blanks from the list below. Who inspected the broken-down walls? _____ Who was ready to do the work when Nehemiah spoke with them? _____ Who were the mockers and discouragers? _____ Who were the builders counting on to give them success?

_____ **SANBALLAT & TOBIAH**

NEHEMIAH   JEWS & RULERS

THE GOD OF HEAVEN

make your Choice

I have recently been discouraged about _____but with God's help I can_____

_____. 111

TAKE THE challenge

check it out!

BIG jobs take LOTS of people.

Check out this exciting chapter and see what you can learn. What gate did the priests work on? _____ Did any women work? _____ How many gates can you count in these sixteen verses? _____ Can you list at least three of them?

_____   _____

_____ Was everyone willing to work?

_____ (v. 5)

make your Choice

God, show me my part in Your work and help me do it well! I believe my part today is_____

_____

_____

THURSDAY NEHEMIAH 3:17-32

TAKE THE challenge

check it out!

Can one person really make a difference?

Notice how many people were repairing in front of their own houses! _____ and Hashub (v. 23) The p _____s (v.28) M_____ (v. 30) Many times, by keeping our own lives "tidy," we can make a huge difference by our example of obedience!

make your Choice

What are some areas of my own life ("house") that need to be worked on and cleaned up a bit? _____

_____

FRIDAY NEHEMIAH 4:1-9

TAKE THE challenge

check it out!

Should we be surprised if not everyone is as excited about our project as we are?

How did Sanballat feel about the rebuilding of the wall? _____

What small animal did Tobiah say could easily break down the wall? _____

How did the people work so they could "keep on keeping on"? (v. 6b)

_____ (v. 9) P_____

(un)to our _____ and posted a guard _____ and _____.

make your Choice

Right now, someone is discouraging me from _____

_____. Lord, help me to "keep on keeping on" doing what I know is right, even when I don't feel like it.

SATURDAY NEHEMIAH 4:10-23

TAKE THE challenge

check it out!

When is it right to fight?

What did the enemies want to do? (v. 11)

_____

On the three big blocks of the "wall" below, write the three important things Nehemiah told all the people to do.

make your Choice

Write down Nehemiah's very confident shout of exclamation at the very end of verse 20: "Our_____

_____ us!" Now write out the Apostle Paul's similar exclamation in Philippians 4:13 (N.T.): "_____!"   113

chart your course

The Wall around Jerusalem was completed in JUST 52 DAYS! In spite of the obstacles of poverty, mockery, fatigue, financial injustice, discouragement, political unrest, and even military threats, God's project - done by God's people - was completed in God's time!

SUNDAY
NEHEMIAH 5:1-13

TAKE THE challenge

check it out!

Do you know what it's like to have nothing to eat, nowhere to live, and only the clothing you are wearing?

Fill in the verse number that describes how poor some of the Jewish people were.

____They borrowed money to pay their taxes.

____Their sons and daughters were sold as slaves.

____They mortgaged their land to buy food.

What did Nehemiah say about this? (v. 9)

_____ What did the people say they would do with the money they had gotten by dishonest or ungodly means (in verse 12)? _____

_____

make your Choice

Do I remember a time when I may have gotten some money by doing something that was dishonest or unkind - maybe by taking advantage of someone else younger or smaller? YES / NO Do I need to confess this and deal with it? _____

MONDAY NEHEMIAH 5:14-6:9

TAKE THE challenge

check it out!

Do you ever get distracted from something important by something that is less important?

Nehemiah's enemies asked for a meeting. Find his reply to them and write it here:"_____

_____

_____

_____" How many times did they try to distract him

from his work? _____ (v. 5)

make your **Choice**

The MOST IMPORTANT things that I need to do every day are:

_____.

Things I need to say "NO" to in order to get those important

things done are_____

_____

TUESDAY NEHEMIAH 6:10-19

TAKE THE challenge

check it out!

Are you ever tempted to hide because you are afraid of people?

ACROSS
1. Where Shemaiah wanted to meet Nehemiah
3. These were sent by Tobiah to frighten Nehemiah (v 19)
4. They wanted _____ to be afraid (intimidated or frightened)
6. Number of days it took to complete the wall

DOWN
2. Lost their confidence when they finally recognized God at work (v.16)
5. When Shemaiah said the men were coming to kill Nehemiah

make your **Choice**

I am afraid right now because of _____

_____.

Lord, help me remember how You helped Nehemiah!

115

WEDNESDAY NEHEMIAH 8:1-12

TAKE THE challenge

check it out!

What is your response to the Word of God?

For at least six hours the people listened as God's Word was read and taught. Search for words that describe their varied responses.

```
E Y E M J W N W S D Z S C
V N V S T R E N G T H T V
I V I D H L M E D E W O B
T H T G N E A T S C J O Y
N K N N X Z T K I E D P
E N E I A A G S D A N W O
T U T P B R T E F W E G T
A T T E N T I V E D V V K
U N D E R S T A N D I N G
K N Y W O R S H I P E D J
```

AMEN JOY ATTENTIVE
BOWED STOOD STRENGTH
UNDERSTANDING
WEEPING WORSHIPED

make your Choice

When I finish my Quiet Time, I:

☐ Am glad to be finished. ☐ Want to learn more.

THURSDAY NEHEMIAH 8:13-9:3

TAKE THE challenge

check it out!

What holidays do you celebrate and WHY do you celebrate them?

The holiday celebrated in this passage was to remember how God cared for the Israelites while they wandered in the wilderness for forty years. How did they celebrate? They lived in _____ _____. They separated themselves from _____. One fourth of the day, they _____.One fourth of the day they _____.

My favorite holiday is _____ _____. One thing that I do on that day that honors

make your Choice

God is _____.

116

FRIDAY NEHEMIAH 12:27-43

check it out!

Is music an important part of worship?

What kind of musical groups did you find in this passage: _____

_____

What was the occasion for celebration? (v. 27)

_____

After each of the two choirs had sung from the wall, all went into the

_____ of _____ and then "o_____ g_____

s_____" and "r_____" with great joy in God!

make your Choice

How much effort do you put into music to glorify God? I will sing with _____ the next time I have the opportunity to glorify God with my singing. If I play an instrument, I will practice _____ minutes every day for God's glory!

SATURDAY NEHEMIAH 13:1-14

TAKE THE challenge

check it out!

When no one is watching, do you do what you are supposed to do anyway?

Where was Nehemiah? (v. 6) _____

_____ Two bad things

happened while he was gone: 1) The enemy of the

Jews (_____) was given a room in the

temple. 2) The Levites were not being supported,

so they had gone to work in their _____.

make your Choice

I know God sees what I do, so even when my parents or teachers aren't here with me, I will do _____

_____.

chart your course

And now . . . .

THE REST OF THE STORY!
(by Dr. Luke)

The Book of Luke ends with Jesus returning to Heaven.

The Book of Acts begins with Jesus returning to Heaven.

We call this the "Ascension of Christ," and it happened forty days after His resurrection.

SUNDAY ACTS 1:1-11

TAKE THE challenge

Christ left His followers with a challenging assignment, AND the power to carry it out!

check it out!

WHAT was the assignment?_____

_____ **WHO** would give them

the power to do this?_____

WHERE were they to wait to receive this power?_____

_____(See also Luke 24:49.)

make your Choice

I will witness to _____ this week,

trusting God's Holy Spirit to help me.

118

MONDAY ACTS 1:12-26

TAKE THE challenge

Decisions, Decisions!! Who really chooses people for leadership?

What did they do first at this meeting (v. 14)?

_____

_____

check it out!

_ Which disciple was gone and needed to be replaced (v. 16)? _____ Who were they trusting to choose the right man (v. 24)?_____

make your Choice

Before I make any decision, I will

_____

and ask God what HIS choice is.

TUESDAY ACTS 2:1-13

TAKE THE challenge

What really happened at Pentecost?

What two tangible symbols of the Holy Spirit were present? 1._____

2._____

check it out!

What were all the believers able to do?_____

_____

Could the people understand them talking about God's works?_____

make your Choice

What in MY life proves that God's Holy Spirit lives in and through me? _____

_____. 119

WEDNESDAY ACTS 2:14-21

TAKE THE challenge

check it out!

Has anyone ever falsely accused you?

Peter defended the believers because the crowd accused them of being _____. What prophet had spoken concerning what people would do when the Holy Spirit came?_____

Peter quoted this prophet to tell them "_____ _____ calls on the name of the Lord shall be saved."

make your Choice

When people falsely accuse me or make fun of me when I talk about God, I will: _____ run away. _____ never talk about God again. _____ keep sharing how they can know God, too.

THURSDAY ACTS 2:22-36

TAKE THE challenge

check it out!

Where can you find the first gospel sermon of the church?

Who was the preacher?_____ (Remember yesterday's Quiet Time?)

To whom was the sermon preached?_____

What did it tell about Jesus?

- His M_____ (v. 22)
- His D_____ (v. 23, 24)
- His R_____ (vv. 24,31)
- His fulfillment of the prophecy of King _____ (v. 25)

make your Choice

In every sermon I hear, I will listen carefully for truth about J_____ C_____.

FRIDAY ACTS 2:37-47

TAKE THE challenge

check it out!

What do you know about the early church?

How did you "get in"? R_____ and be
b_____ How many people joined
the church the first day?_____
In which verses do you see the following activities
of the early church? (Put the verse numbers in
the boxes provided.) Teaching ☐ Fellowship ☐ Eating together ☐
Praising God ☐ Visiting in homes ☐ Sharing ☐

make your Choice

What's one thing I really appreciate about my church and church
family? _____
_____

SATURDAY ACTS 3:1-11

TAKE THE challenge

check it out!

Is money always the best gift?

What did the crippled beggar want from Peter and
John?_____ What did they
give him instead?_____

What three things did the man do in the temple?

1) _____ 2) _____

3) _____

make your Choice

What gifts can I give that cost no money? I can help _____
_____ . I can encourage _____. I can
obey _____ . I can do a chore for _____.
I can smile at_____.

121

wk. 27

weekly passage covered
ACTS 3:12-5:32

chart your course

It's a crazy time in Jerusalem! The temple traditions, sacrifices, and ceremonies are being challenged, having been fulfilled by Jesus Christ, the Messiah. Peter and John remind them what the Old Testament prophets have said about Jesus.

SUNDAY ACTS 3:12-26

TAKE THE challenge

Make sure the right person gets the credit!

check it out!

Did Peter and John accept praise for healing the crippled man?_____ Who really healed the man?_____ Write down every name for God or His Son that you find in these verses: _____

_____ _____ _____

_____ _____

make your Choice

I can give credit to God for the good things that happen to me by

_____.

MONDAY ACTS 4:1-12

TAKE THE Challenge

check it out!

Is there more than one way to be saved?

The rulers were angry because Peter and John

preached about_____. The church

was growing to about _____ men.

Peter and John spent the night in _____.

They told the truth in court: S_____

can only be found through _____ ' name.

make your Choice

In what do people sometimes try to find salvation besides Jesus?

_____

How will I share this truth with others? _____

_____

TUESDAY ACTS 4:13-22

TAKE THE Challenge

check it out!

Can people tell that you have "been with Jesus"?

Were Peter and John highly educated (v. 13)?

_____ What did the people notice

about them (v. 13)?_____

Because they were afraid Peter and John's

message would spread, what did they command

them not to do (v. 18)? _____

_____

make your Choice

When I have my _____ _____ each

day, people are more likely to sense that I have "been with Jesus."

WEDNESDAY ACTS 4:23-37

TAKE THE challenge

check it out!

How can I become bolder in talking about God?

What did the people do when Peter and John were

released? (v.24) _____ their _____ to _____.

In answer to their prayer: (v.31)

The place was _____.

They were filled with the _____ _____.

They spoke _____

make your Choice

Prayerfully, I will share the gospel with _____

today, trusting God to give me boldness (courage).

THURSDAY ACTS 5:1-11

TAKE THE challenge

check it out!

Is God serious when He says that He hates lying?

A _ _ _ _ _ _ _ and S_ _ _ _ _ _ _ _

s_ _ _ a piece of land and told people they were

giving _ _ _ the money to the church. They

really k _ _ _ part of the money for themselves

and fell down d _ _ _ when they lied about it.

make your Choice

I can think of a time when I was not completely truthful.
(YES or NO) To please God, I will do my best to tell the
whole truth all the time. (YES or NO)

124

FRIDAY ACTS 5:12-23

TAKE THE challenge

check it out!

Did you know? God always has a plan!!

1. (down) The apostles performed many signs and _____ among the people.

2. (down) During the night an _____ helped them escape.

2. (across) The angry high priests and Sadducees arrested the _____.

3. (down) The apostles were then instructed to go and stand in the _____.

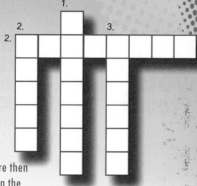

make your Choice

Even when the situation seems _____,

I will __ __ __ __ __ God to work out the details.

SATURDAY ACTS 5:24-32

TAKE THE challenge

check it out!

Is it ever right to disobey a law?

God said, "TEACH."

The Jews said, "D__ __ __ T__ __ __ __ __."

Peter said, "We ought to __ __ __ __ God rather than __ __ __."

make your Choice

In order to obey God, I have to know what He says. Where do I find out what God says about right and wrong? _____

125

wk. 28

chart your course

DID YOU KNOW THAT . . .

The SANHEDRIN was the ruling council of the Jews. It included the HIGH PRIEST, the SADDUCEES, and the PHARISEES. Two well-known Pharisees were NICODEMUS (see John 3) and GAMALIEL (who was the Apostle Paul's teacher).

SUNDAY ACTS 5:33-42

TAKE THE challenge

Do hard times make you feel special? They should!

What did the Sanhedrin want to do to the apostles (v. 33)? _____

Instead, what did they do (v. 40)? _____

_____

check it out!

What was the attitude of the apostles when they left the Sanhedrin (v. 41)? _____

Did they keep teaching?_____

make your Choice

I would be glad to suffer for the cause of Christ, just like the _____ did. When bad times come, I will (check one) ☐ run away ☐ keep on serving God cheerfully.

MONDAY ACTS 6:1-15

check it out!

Did you know that there is an important job for everyone in the church?

Put a check mark by the tasks that took up most of the apostles' time.

__ Daily food distribution
__ Prayer
__ Serving tables
__ Ministry of the Word

Circle the tasks that they chose wise men to help them with.

make your
Choice

No matter what job God chooses me for, I will do my very
_____ for His glory!

TUESDAY ACTS 7:1-16

TAKE THE
challenge

check it out!

Sometimes we need to be reminded of what God has done in the past.

Fill in the names of the men from the Old Testament that Stephen spoke about.

_____ God told him to leave his country.

_____ Father of the twelve patriarchs

_____ Sold as a slave into Egypt

_____ King of Egypt

make your
Choice

What do I want to be remembered for someday? _____
_____
_____ 127

WEDNESDAY ACTS 7:17-29

Are God's chosen leaders always accepted by the people they lead?

Stephen continues to speak about how the Jews treated God's chosen leaders. How long did Moses live in his father's house?_____

Who raised him after that?_____

When he went back to his own people, did they accept his leadership?_____

make your Choice

Some of the leaders in my life are:_____
_____ How do I treat them? a) I accept and respect them as leaders from God... or b) I complain, disobey, or disrespect them.

THURSDAY ACTS 7:30-43

TAKE THE challenge

Your Sunday school lessons are more than just "Bible stories"!

check it out!

Who is still preaching in the passage? _____
(See Acts 6:8.) How long did Moses wait in the wilderness before God spoke to him? _____

make your Choice

From this "Bible story" about Moses, I should learn to w_____ on God until I hear His direction, even if it seems like a long time.

FRIDAY ACTS 7:44-60

TAKE THE challenge

check it out!

Has anyone ever thrown rocks at you?

Who was the "Righteous One" or "Just One" that Stephen said they had murdered?_____

Stephen, even in this terrible moment of death, was _____ with the _____ _____. He was enabled to see right into _____, and saw _____ standing where? _____ Was Stephen angry at his murderers? YES / NO

Stephen was the first Christian MARTYR.

make your ChoIce

When someone hurts me for telling the truth, I should (Circle the letter of the correct one.)
a. Pray for him.
b. Forgive him before he asks.
c. Try to get back at him.

SATURDAY ACTS 8:1-13

TAKE THE challenge

check it out!

Have you ever moved to a different school or a different city?

Why did the people of the church have to leave

Jerusalem (v. 1)? _____

Who moved to Samaria? _____

What did he do there?_____

_____

make your ChoIce

One hard place I'm in right now is: _____

_____. Lord, help me remember that no matter where I am, You have me there for a special reason.

chart your course

In Acts 1:8, Jesus said the believers would be witnesses in:

Jerusalem   **JUDEA**

Samaria

All over the earth

Acts chapter 8, the Gospel was shared with people from: Jerusalem - verse 1, Judea - verse 1, Samaria - verse 5 and in Ethiopia (a country in Africa) - verse 27 AMEN!!

SUNDAY   ACTS 8:14-25

TAKE THE challenge

Can giving money help you gain God's approval or His gifts?

Was Simon a believer (v. 21)?

_____

What did he want to buy (v. 19)?

_____

Peter said Simon's

_____

was not right.

check it out!

make your Choice

What is your true attitude? (Check one.)

- [ ] I don't give anything because Jesus doesn't want my money.
- [ ] I happily give an offering, not expecting anything in return.
- [ ] I give money to the church so that God will bless me.

TAKE THE challenge

Can you find Jesus in the Old Testament?

check it out!

What book of the Bible was the man in the chariot reading?_____ What did Philip tell him about, from the very same Scripture?_____

_____

What did the man do after he understood and believed in Jesus?_____

_____

make your Choice

Check all that are true.

☐ I have believed in Jesus as my Savior.

☐ I have been baptized.

☐ I need to talk to someone about how I can be saved or baptized.

TAKE THE challenge

Sometimes God uses drastic measures to get our attention!

check it out!

How did Saul treat Christians?_____

_____

On the way to Damascus:

he SAW_____.

he HEARD _____.

his EYES BECAME _____.

make your Choice

Which is true about you?

☐ I read my Bible every day, paying attention to what God is saying to me.

☐ I only read my Bible and pay attention in church if I'm going through a tough time and need God's help.

TAKE THE challenge

check it out!

Should we form an opinion about someone based on what we hear about them from others?

Had Ananias heard good or bad things about Saul?

_____ What did God say about Saul?

"He is a ___ ___ ___ ___ ___ ___ vessel (or

instrument)." What did Saul do immediately after

receiving his sight back (v. 20)? _____

make your Choice

Before I form a bad opinion about someone, I will watch to see

what _____ does in his/her life.

TAKE THE challenge

check it out!

What are friends for? Read about an escape in a basket!

What did the Jews in Damascus try to do to

Saul?_____

Did the believers in Jerusalem accept Saul?

_____

Who went with Saul to share his testimony with

the apostles?_____

make your Choice

What is one way I can stand up for Jesus like Barnabas stood

up for Saul?_____

_____

132

FRIDAY ACTS 9:32-43

check it out!

What was the purpose of miracles?

What was the name of the paralyzed man who was healed?_____ What two names are given for the seamstress that was raised from the dead? _____and_____ What do verses 35 and 42 tell us happened after each of these miracles? _____

make your Choice

What is the greatest miracle that God has done in MY life?

_____

_____

SATURDAY ACTS 10:1-8

check it out!

To what kind of person does God speak?

Circle the words that describe Cornelius.

STINGY   **Prayerful**

Mocking   **GENEROUS**

GOD-HONORING   **Neglectful**

Who spoke to Cornelius?_____
Who was he instructed to call?_____

make your Choice

I will _____ for God to speak to me each day by reading the _____ and being an obedient, attentive Christian.

133

chart your course

The book of Acts is all about...
TRANSITION or CHANGE . . .

From LAW to GRACE
From TEMPLE to CHURCH
From SABBATH to SUNDAY
From UNCLEAN to CLEAN
From SEPARATED to JOINED TOGETHER
From JEW vs. GENTILE to CHRISTIANS

What made this change possible?
The CROSS of JESUS CHRIST!!

SUNDAY ACTS 10:9-22

TAKE THE challenge

Do you ever think that you
know better than God?

Circle the correct choice for each statement:

Peter was   **HUNGRY / THIRSTY.**

The animals were in a   **CAGE / SHEET.**

Peter didn't want to eat the animals because they

were   **CUTE / UNCLEAN.**

God had made the animals   **CLEAN / FRIENDLY.**

check it out!

make your Choice

Which is more important: what I think about something or
what God thinks about something?

TAKE THE challenge

check it out!

How do you respond to God's messengers?

1. Peter went to Cornelius' house because:
a. he was invited.
b. God told him to go.
c. both of the above reasons.

2. Cornelius:
a. had his servants prepare a meal.
b. washed Peter's feet and gave him a meal.
c. gathered everyone together to listen.

make your Choice

When someone is teaching God's Word, I will:
(check all that apply)

____ Follow along in my Bible ____ Daydream ____ Take notes

____ Pass notes to my friends ____ Listen attentively

TAKE THE challenge

check it out!

What do you need to tell people so that they can be saved?

Fill in the verse numbers where Peter tells about:

Christ's death: verse [   ]

Jesus raised on the third day: verse [   ]

Forgiveness of sins: verse [   ]

Believing in Him: verse [   ]

make your Choice

I can tell _____ how to be

saved because HE / SHE needs Jesus as HIS / HER Savior.

WEDNESDAY ACTS 11:1-15

Is it okay to be friends with people who don't do everything just the way we do?

CIRCUMCISION - a Jewish ritual symbolizing separation to God that Gentiles did not participate in. Peter, who was a Jewish believer, was criticized by Jews because he ate with whom?_____

check it out!

Who sent Peter to these people (v. 12)? _____

Did they receive the Holy Spirit (v. 15)? _____

make your Choice

God may send me to people who are:
(Circle the letter of the correct answer.)
A. LIKE ME.   B. NOT LIKE ME.   C. BOTH

THURSDAY ACTS 11:16-30

TAKE THE challenge

Has anyone ever called you a different name (nickname), rather than your real name?

Were the people in Antioch Jews, Gentiles (Greeks) or both?_____

What were the believers in the church of Antioch called?_____ "Ian" means "belonging to," so "Christian" means "belonging to _____."

check it out!

make your Choice

How do I live up to the name "Christian"? _____

_____

FRIDAY ACTS 12:1-11

TAKE THE challenge

Is being a Christian always easy?

Peter was put in [ ] _ _ _ _ _ _

James was killed with a _ _ _ [ ] _

Peter was bound with _ _ [ ] _ _ _

The church met in the house of _ _ _ [ ] (v. 12)

Check out the letters in the circles!

check it out!

make your ChOjce

In good times and bad, I will choose to _ _ _ _ !!

SATURDAY ACTS 12:12-25

TAKE THE challenge

When you pray, do you expect God to answer?

check it out!

Who answered the door when Peter

knocked? _____

What was her reaction? _____

The people didn't _____

her. When they saw Peter, they were _____.

make your ChOjce

When God answers my prayers, I am: (Check all that are true.)
____ surprised. ____ joyful. ____ thankful. ____ indifferent.

137

chart your course

Lystra

Derbe

Antioch

As you do your Quiet Time this week, look in the back of your Bible or the family Bible and see if it has a map of Paul's Missionary Journeys. You will be able to see these important cities he visited even closer on a bigger map. Follow their journeys each day!

SUNDAY ACTS 13:1-13

TAKE THE challenge

check it out!

Want to know God's will?
Stay busy!

God called Saul and Barnabas to be missionaries

while they were doing what? _____ and

_____ How did they travel?_____

Who was their helper?_____

What was Saul's name changed to?_____

make your Choice

While I am waiting to see what God wants me to do when I grow up, I can serve Him by _____

_____

_____.

MONDAY ACTS 13:14-25

TAKE THE challenge

If God was to write a story about you, how would He describe YOUR life?

List at least four Old Testament characters in Paul's first missionary sermon: (1)_____

(2) _____ (3) _____

(4) _____ (5) _____

How did God describe David? A man after

_____ _____ _____

check it out!

make your ChOice

What is one thing I need to change if I'm going to truly be God's person? _____

TUESDAY ACTS 13:26-41

TAKE THE challenge

Did you know that Paul had the same Old Testament that we do?

check it out!

In verse 33, which Psalm was Paul quoting?

_____ Look at Psalm 2:7.

Was Paul right about what it says?_____

To whom is this verse referring?_____

What is my favorite Psalm in the Bible? _____

make your ChOice

Why? _____

_____

TAKE THE challenge

Attitude is everything!

check it out!

What was the Jews' ATTITUDE toward Paul's ministry (v. 45)?_____ What was the Gentiles' ATTITUDE toward the Word of God (v. 48)?_____ What was the disciples' ATTITUDE about their persecution (v. 52)?_____

make your Choice

I want to be _____ toward God's Word. I want to be _____ when God takes me through tough times.

TAKE THE challenge

How do you react when someone says bad things about you to others?

check it out!

Beside each of the cities Paul visits in today's Quiet Time passage, put the verse numbers that identify them: v._____ Iconium v. _____ Lystra v. _____ Derbe. What did they plan to do to them (v. 5)? _____ What did Paul and Barnabas continue to do (v. 7)? _____

_____

_____

make your Choice

When others misjudge me, or speak badly about me, I will:
_____ continue doing what is right.
_____ quit trying.

140

FRIDAY ACTS 14:14-28

TAKE THE challenge

check it out!

How quickly people can change their minds!

Why were Paul and Barnabas so upset?
Because the people were treating them like
_____ (See verses 11-13.)
The next thing they knew, the people were so
angry that they_____ Paul and left him
for dead (v. 19). Did they quit doing God's work?
_____

make your ChOice

I will value _____'s opinion of my efforts more than
_____'s opinion.

SATURDAY ACTS 15:1-12

TAKE THE challenge

check it out!

Do you have to dress a certain way, cut your hair a certain way, or go through a special ceremony to be saved?

What did the men from Judea say that you had
to do to be saved (v. 1)? _____
(This is a special ceremony in which Jewish men
demonstrate their faith.) Did the Pharisees agree
(v. 5)? _____ Did Paul and Barnabas
agree (vv. 10-11)? _____ How are we
saved (v. 11)? Through _____

make your ChOice

I will not jump to conclusions about another's salvation based on:
(check all that are true) ____ How many earrings they wear
____ How they dress ____ What music they like
____ What church they go to

chart your course

Syria · Antioch

Continue to follow the missionary journeys of Paul and Barnabas in this week's Quiet Time passages. You can see the outline of where they went, starting at Antioch in Syria at the right of the map.

SUNDAY ACTS 15:13-29

TAKE THE Challenge

check it out!

Did you know that God uses AMBASSADORS?

AMBASSADOR — *an official representative sent from one country to another*

What two men did the Jerusalem church choose to send to Antioch with Paul and Barnabas? _____ and _____ Check out verse 32 to see what they did while they were there: _____

_____

make your Choice

I can be an ambassador or a peacemaker today by _____

_____.

MONDAY ACTS 15:30-41

TAKE THE challenge

check it out!

Do godly people ever disagree?

What did Paul and Barnabas disagree about?

_____

How did they resolve this issue? Barnabas took

_____ and Paul took _____.

Then they went their separate ways to minister.

make your Choice

What unimportant disagreements do I allow to keep me from

serving God and others?_____

_____

TUESDAY ACTS 16:1-13

TAKE THE challenge

check it out!

Does God ever change your plans?

What two places did Paul try to go, but was

hindered by the Spirit? Verse 6 : A_____

Verse 7: B_____ Do we know how the

Spirit directed him?_____ How did God

direct him to go to Macedonia?_____

make your Choice

How does God's Spirit teach and guide me in making godly

choices? _____

_____

143

WEDNESDAY ACTS 16:14-24

TAKE THE challenge

check it out!

Do you always get praise and encouragement when you do something for the Lord?

Name the two people in this passage that Paul was able to help by sharing Jesus with them.

_____and _____

Verse 23 tells us which reward they received for their work. They were _____ and thrown into _____.

make your Choice

When doing something for God or others I should:

◻ expect to be praised and thanked.

◻ expect some people to criticize and misunderstand.

THURSDAY ACTS 16:25-40

TAKE THE challenge

check it out!

Which is a more effective witnessing tool: Whining? Or Rejoicing?

Circle the correct answers.

What were Paul and Silas doing in prison?

WHINING OR REJOICING?

What disaster happened in the jail?

AN EARTHQUAKE OR A FIRE?

What happened to the jailer?

HE WAS KILLED OR HE WAS SAVED?

make your Choice

Lord, in difficult circumstances, please help me to:

◻ *Complain and whine.* ◻ *Trust You and rejoice.*

144

FRIDAY ACTS 17:1-9

TAKE THE challenge

Is serving God always easy?

check it out!

How many weeks did Paul teach about Christ in the synagogue?_____ Did many believe? _____ The Jews who did NOT believe started a _____ in Thessalonica (Can you find this city on your map?).

make your Choice

I am willing to work hard and suffer persecution to share Christ with others.
Signature: _____

SATURDAY ACTS 17:10-21

TAKE THE challenge

How do you spend your time?

check it out!

What did the BEREANS spend their time doing (v. 11)? Studying the _____ every _____

What did the ATHENIANS spend their time doing (v. 21)? Telling or hearing something _____

make your Choice

Circle the letter of the statement that is more important:
A. Buying CDs, magazines, and movies to keep up with the latest trends   B. Studying the Bible every day to get to know God's heart

145

chart your course

Paul preached to unsaved Jews in their SYNAGOGUES on SATURDAY (the Sabbath). Paul preached to believers in their HOUSES on SUNDAY because they met together on the first day of the week to celebrate Christ's resurrection. WHEN and WHERE do YOU meet to worship?

SUNDAY ACTS 17:22-34

TAKE THE challenge

Do "religious" activities bring people to God?

The altar in verse 23 was built to whom? "to an

_____ _____"

List the verse number (Write it in the box provided.) in which Paul describes the true God as: Creator _____ Giver of Life _____ Planner of men's lives _____ Judge _____ What does this true God command all men to do if they want to know Him (v. 30)? _____

check it out!

make your Choice

What is one way in this week that I can let others know I worship the TRUE GOD? _____

_____

MONDAY ACTS 18:1-17

Does God know His people before they know Him?

What group of people opposed and mistreated Paul in Corinth?_____ To which group of people did he go next to share the gospel? _____ God encouraged Paul by saying, "I have _____ people in this city." How long did Paul stay and teach?_____

make your Choice

Since only God knows who is going to accept Him, I should share the gospel with _____.

TUESDAY ACTS 18:18-28

Can your home be a place of ministry?

To what place did Aquila and Priscilla move?

_____

What bold preacher also came to that city after Paul moved on?_____
(v 26) When Aquila and Priscilla heard him they explained to him _____ _____ of _____ more _____.

make your Choice

When friends come to my home it is more important for me to: (circle one)   A. ENTERTAIN THEM.   B. ENCOURAGE THEM

WEDNESDAY ACTS 19:1-10

TAKE THE challenge

check it out!

Did you know . . . your response to God's Word may influence your opportunities to hear the Word?

How did the Jews in the synagogue respond to Paul's teaching?_____ How long did he speak there? _____

How did the disciples in the hall of Tyrannus respond to Paul's teaching? _____

How long did he teach there?_____

make your Choice

Whenever I have an opportunity to hear God's Word, I will

_____.

THURSDAY ACTS 19:11-22

TAKE THE challenge

check it out!

Have you ever played with games like Ouija boards or tarot cards, or read books about warlocks or witches?

What happened to the Jews who tried to use Jesus' name to drive out evil spirits?_____

_____ When people became believers, what did they do with all their books about sorcery and magical arts?_____

_____

make your Choice

In order to please my Savior, I need to get rid of any books, CDs, or games that are connected to witchcraft. List them here, and check this box when you get rid of them. ☐

148

FRIDAY ACTS 19:23-41

TAKE THE challenge

check it out!

People get very emotional about their salary and the economy. (Just watch the news!)

By preaching against idols, Paul was interfering

with the business of _____.

This caused a great _____

(parade or riot)

in Ephesus!

make your Choice

If I had to choose between two activities, I would pick:

_____ An opportunity to make some money

_____ An opportunity to serve God or help others

SATURDAY ACTS 20:1-12

TAKE THE challenge

check it out!

How long are you willing to listen to a preacher preach?

What day of the week did they meet together (v. 7)?

_____

How long did Paul preach? _____

What happened to Eutychus? _____

What miracle did God do? _____

make your Choice

To pay better attention in my church's one-hour services, I will:

_____ pass notes to my friends. _____ take notes on the message.

_____ follow along in my Bible.

149

chart your course

Paul is now near the end of his life as a free man, and he knows it. In spite of the fact that he knows he will lose his freedom, and very possibly his life, he follows God's direction to go to Jerusalem, trusting God's great plan.

SUNDAY ACTS 20:13-24

TAKE THE challenge

check it out!

What is your life worth?

Paul talks about the two things necessary for

salvation in verse 21: R_____ toward

God (a change of mind). F_____ in Jesus

Christ. He says his life is worth nothing except to

fulfill the task of testifying to the g_____ of

the g_____ of G_____.

make your choice

I want my life to be worth something! I can testify of God's grace this week: Where?_____

When?_____ To whom?_____

150

TAKE THE challenge

How would you say goodbye to someone you knew you would never see again?

check it out!

Look back at verse 17. To whom was Paul saying goodbye? The elders at _____.

Match the following to complete Paul's instructions.

___1. warning   a. hard

___2. work   b. against false teachers

___3. be shepherds   c. the weak

___4. support or help   d. of the church

make your Choice

I want my friends to remember me as someone who

_____.

TAKE THE challenge

Are you willing to obey God even when your friends say you are wrong?

check it out!

Verses 4 and 12 say that Paul's friends urged him

not to do what?_____

Paul's reply was that he was ready to _____

_____

for the name of the Lord Jesus.

make your Choice

I believe that God's plan for me is perfect. I will obey Him, even if others _____

_____.

151

WEDNESDAY ACTS 21:15-26

Are you willing to go above and beyond to maintain a good testimony?

Verse 19: Missionary report: God has done great

things among the G_____.

Verse 20: Potential problem: offending the

J_____ by departing from Jewish customs.

Verses 23 and 24: Solution: Paul should go through the Jewish

purification ceremony to show respect for the _____.

make your Choice

Although some rules about clothing, music, and haircuts may

seem silly to me, I will _____

them so I don't hinder the gospel or Christian fellowship.

THURSDAY ACTS 21:27-40

TAKE THE challenge

Sometimes people are offended in spite of our best efforts to "keep the peace."

check it out!

Who seized Paul and
stirred up the crowd
against him?

_____

Who arrested Paul?

_____

make your Choice

I know that I cannot please "all people all of the time," but I

will always try to please _____.

FRIDAY ACTS 22:1-16

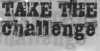

TAKE THE challenge

check it out!

Have you ever shared your testimony?

TESTIMONY: *a declaration of events as witnessed or experienced by an individual.*

What event was Paul giving testimony of in this passage?_____

_____

make your Choice

What is MY testimony of my salvation?_____

_____

_____

SATURDAY ACTS 22:17-30

TAKE THE challenge

check it out!

Does your citizenship matter?

What did the commander order to be done to

Paul?_____ When they found

out that Paul was a citizen of Rome, what did they

do?_____

make your Choice

As a child of God, I am a citizen of _____ (See Philippians 3:20.) and can trust God to protect me.

153

chart your course

PAUL'S TRIALS:

Before the Sanhedrin in Jerusalem

Before Felix in Caesarea

(Two years in prison)

Before Festus in Caesarea

Before Agrippa in Caesarea

(Shipwrecked on Malta)

(Two years house arrest in Rome)

SUNDAY ACTS 23:1-10

TAKE THE challenge

Does arguing among ourselves usually accomplish anything?

check it out!

SANHEDRIN: *The religious ruling group of the Jews, made up of the Sadducees, who believe there is no_____, no_____, and no_____(v. 8), and the Pharisees, who believe in all three!*

What happened when Paul brought up the subject of the resurrection in verse 9?_____ Did they accomplish their purpose of determining Paul's guilt or innocence?_____

make your Choice

God, when I'm tempted to argue, help me to remember that arguing generally accomplishes _____

_____.

MONDAY ACTS 23:11-22

TAKE THE challenge

When should I talk about a secret that I overhear?

check it out!

Who overheard the plot to kill Paul?_____

Who did he tell first?_____

Who did he tell second?_____

Did he tell anyone else?_____

make your CHOICE

When I overhear something, I will

____ gossip about it to everyone I see.

____ report it to the person involved, only if it will prevent someone from getting hurt.

TUESDAY ACTS 23:23-35

TAKE THE challenge

How many soldiers does it take to rescue someone in danger?

Can you figure out how many Romans it took to get Paul safely to Caesarea?

check it out!

_____ **SOLDIERS** + _____ **HORSEMEN** +

_____ **SPEARMEN** = _____ **TOTAL**

make your CHOICE

Thank you, Lord, for the protection that you provide through our government. I will pray for our leaders. Write the names of three government leaders here: _____

_____

WEDNESDAY ACTS 24:1-16

TAKE THE challenge

check it out!

Have you ever been accused of doing something you didn't do?

What did Tertullus, the lawyer, accuse Paul of

doing? (vv. 5,6) _____

_____

What did Paul say about these charges?_____

_____

make your Choice

When I am falsely accused, I will

____ DEFEND MYSELF IN ANGER.   ____ CALMLY TELL THE TRUTH.

THURSDAY ACTS 24:17-27

TAKE THE challenge

check it out!

What have you had to WAIT for recently? Was it hard to WAIT?

Paul was kept under guard by a C_____,

but not in prison. Who sent for Paul often to hear

what he had to say? _____

How long was Paul a prisoner of Felix? _____

_____

(But Paul got to share the gospel all that time!)

make your Choice

The next time I am waiting a long time for something, I will ask, "What is God trying to accomplish through this time?" I am waiting on God for _____.

FRIDAY ACTS 25:1-12

TAKE THE challenge

Did the Apostle Paul believe in the death penalty?

check it out!

Before whom was Paul tried? _____

Where did the Jews want Paul to be tried? _____

_____ To whom did Paul

appeal?_____ Did he refuse

to die if he was found guilty? _____

make your Choice

The next time I hear debate over the death penalty, I will

remember that _____ acknowledged that God

gave the government authority to punish certain crimes by death.

SATURDAY ACTS 25:13-27

TAKE THE challenge

Why in the world is Paul on trial?

check it out!

Paul is to be sent to Rome to appear before

C_____(v. 21).

Does Festus know what charges to bring against him?

_____ (v. 26)

Who is there to help write specific charges against

Paul? _____ (v. 26)

make your Choice

I understand that I may be _____ accused of

doing something wrong. Jesus was, and so was Paul.

chart your course

Do you ever wonder what Paul did during his two years of house arrest in Rome? The rest of the New Testament gives us clues. He wrote the books of Philippians, Ephesians, Colossians, and Philemon! He was probably released, then imprisoned again, and eventually beheaded because of the stand which he took for Christ!

SUNDAY ACTS 26:1-18

TAKE THE challenge

Once again, Paul shares his TESTIMONY!

check it out!

Who gave Paul permission to share his testimony? _____ His testimony included three things: 1. What his life was like before he was saved: He was a _____. (v. 5) He was an enemy of _____. (v. 9) 2. How he was different after he was saved: He was sent as a _____. (v. 16) 3. A verse that told how he was saved: Verse 18—from darkness to _____ from Satan to _____, to receive _____ of sins.

make your choice

I will sit down this week and write down these three parts of my own testimony so I will be prepared when opportunities come!

MONDAY ACTS 26:19-32

check it out!

Why do preachers give an invitation after their message?

Agrippa heard Paul's testimony and the truth about Christ's death and resurrection, and then Paul asked an important question: "DO YOU

_____?"

make your Choice

I [ ] **DO** [ ] **DO NOT** believe in the death and resurrection of Christ. (Have you asked your friends this question?)

TUESDAY ACTS 27:1-13

TAKE THE challenge

check it out!

Isn't it exciting to start on a trip?

How would you travel to Rome? _____

How did Paul travel to Rome?_____

They had no engines, so they were totally

dependent on what (v. 7)? _____

In this season of the year, sailing was _____

_____(v. 9).

make your Choice

Lord, I am thankful that you make travel so easy for us now, by providing _____, _____, _____, and _____.

159

WEDNESDAY ACTS 27:14-29

check it out!

Can a hurricane mess up God's plan?

Imagine being on the ship with Paul! Circle True (T) or False (F) about the following statements:

T or F They threw things overboard to lighten the ship.

T or F They didn't see the sun or stars for many days.

T or F The sailors gave up hope.

T or F The storm lasted three days.

Was it God's will for Paul to stand trial in Rome before Caesar? _____

make your Choice

Help me to remember, Lord, that

__ __ __ __ __ __ __

can keep Your will from being done, even a 14-day hurricane!

THURSDAY ACTS 27:30-44

check it out!

Have you ever been so busy or worried that you forgot to eat?

Why did Paul encourage them to eat? _____

_____

What did he stop to do before he ate? _____

_____

How many people were on the ship?_____

_____

How many people made it safely to shore? _____

_____

make your Choice

At my next meal, I will stop to _____ God, and remember that the food I eat is a gift from God that I need in order to stay physically strong.

FRIDAY ACTS 28:1-16

TAKE THE challenge

Hospitality - generous and kind treatment of guests.

How did the island people show hospitality to Paul and his friends?_____

How did Publius show hospitality?_____

How did Paul feel when the Christians at Puteoli showed him hospitality? _____

_____

make your choice

I can show hospitality today to _____.

(Hint: Think of anyone God may bring into your path!!)

SATURDAY ACTS 28:17-31

TAKE THE challenge

HOSPITALITY = OPPORTUNITIES TO SHARE CHRIST!

Whom did Paul invite to his house?

Verse 17_____

Verse 23_____

Verse 30_____

What did he do while they were there (v. 31)?

_____

make your choice

When I am with people, my primary goal should be:

A. TO HAVE FUN.

B. TO ENTERTAIN AND IMPRESS THEM.

C. TO FIND A WAY TO SHARE CHRIST.

161

chart your course

The Book of Numbers *is the fourth book of Moses —* Genesis Exodus **LEVITICUS** NUMBERS *DEUTERONOMY.*

*It is called "*Numbers*" because twice in the book the whole nation of Israel was counted (chapters 1 and 26). It tells the story of Israel's 40-year wandering in the wilderness.(This was punishment from God because they did not believe and obey Him when He told them to enter and possess the Promised Land!)*

SUNDAY NUMBERS 1:1-4, 44-46

TAKE THE challenge

Is God interested in the crowd, or the people in the crowd?

Who was Moses and Aaron asked to number (or count) and record? _____

Who was to help count? _____ man _____ e_____ t_____

check it out!

All the Israelites who were _____ years old or older and were able to serve in the Israeli (circle one)
COLLEGES / ARMY / AIR FORCE

make your choice

Who was to help count?
_____ man _____ e_____ t_____

TAKE THE challenge

check it out!

Do you ever get tired of a job you have been given?

The Levites were not counted as part of the army because they had been given a specific job. What was it? (v. 50) _____ _____ Do you think that they ever got tired of always being the ones to set up and clean up the tabernacle every single time?

_____

make your Choice

What job do you really get tired of? _____
Does it make a difference that your job gets done? _____
God, help me to faithfully _____
with a servant's heart for You!

TAKE THE challenge

check it out!

What kind of people does God choose to serve Him?

In this passage, find the people and groups of people that God set aside for special services.

```
I L E V I T E S A K Y N
T S D L M Z T T A Q B R
H K R T W E H S R R N O
A R I A E V A E O F C B
M E U I E D M I N W K T
A I R U V L A R O E M S
R P F B A D I P E O T R
R A L V V A X T S W Q I
I T B A D A N E E F T F
A B I H U A S Z H S A P
```

AARON   ABIHU
FIRSTBORN   ISRAELITES
ITHAMAR   LEVITE
NADAB   MOSES   PRIESTS

make your Choice

What special job does God have for me to do? _____

_____

Lord, I'm ready! Please show me what to do today!

WEDNESDAY NUMBERS 3:38-51

TAKE THE challenge

check it out!

Has anyone ever taken your place before?

Who took the place of all the firstborn who belonged to God in Israel? _____

What did the families who didn't have a Levite to take the place of their firstborn have to do to "redeem" their firstborn? Pay _____ shekels.

make your Choice

Who took my place so I don't have to die for my sins?_____
_____ - Who can I tell about this today?_____

THURSDAY NUMBERS 6:1-8, 22-27

TAKE THE challenge

check it out!

How important is it to keep your promises?

A Nazarite makes a special promise to God to separate himself to God by: - Not eating or drinking (circle one) KOOL-AID / ROOT BEER / ANY ALCOHOLIC DRINK OF ANY KIND - Not eating anything from the (circle one): ORCHARD / GRAPE VINE / CABBAGE PATCH - Not cutting his _____ - Not going near any thing or person that is _____

[There were two people in the Bible whose parents made this promise for them before they were born: John the Baptist (who kept the promise) and Samson (who did not keep the promise).]

make your Choice

What promise have YOU made to God?_____
_____ I need to do a better job keeping my promise to_____.

FRIDAY NUMBERS 7:1-9, 84-89

TAKE THE challenge

check it out!

Are there practical things that are needed for God's work to be successful?

What did the leaders bring as gifts in verse 3?

_____ In verse 84?

12 each of _____, _____ and _____

In verse 87? 12 each of these sacrificial animals:

_____, _____, and _____ What practical things

might your church need for a VBS ministry? _____

What might a camp need? _____

make your Choice

Lord, I could give _____

_____ to Your work

SATURDAY NUMBERS 8:5-18

TAKE THE challenge

check it out!

What can you do to prepare to serve God?

Count how many times in this passage you find a word that means "clean" ("cleanse") or "purify" or "wash" [   ]. Verse 11 tells us WHY the Levites were being prepared in this manner: "That they may _____

_____

_____."

Look up these verses to see how YOU can GET CLEAN so you are ready to serve God– Psalm 119:9 and 1 John 1:9

make your Choice

Every day I want to let God cleanse me by _____

_____ and _____

_____.

165

weekly passage covered
NUMBERS 8:19-13:25

chart your course

ATONEMENT *is the restoring of God's relationship with man. If you take this long word and break it down into parts, it might look like this:* at-one-ment. *God's atonement makes a person at one with Him through the sacrifice of His Son, Jesus, on the cross. In the Old Testament, God gave his people pictures of atonement - like sacrifices and cleansing ceremonies - that acted as substitutes for their sins so they could be at one with Him again.*

SUNDAY — NUMBERS 8:19-26

TAKE THE challenge

check it out!

Who are the special people in your life?

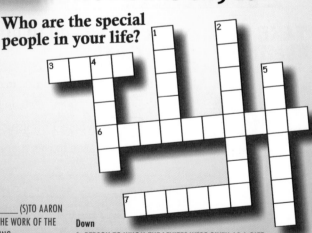

Across
3. THE LEVITES WERE GOD'S _____ (S)TO AARON AND HIS SONS TO HELP WITH THE WORK OF THE TABERNACLE OR TENT OF MEETING.
6. HOW OLD A LEVITE HAD TO BE TO START WORK
7. WHAT THE LEVITES DID TO THEIR CLOTHES

Down
1. PERSON TO WHOM THE LEVITES WERE GIVEN AS A GIFT
2. WHAT THE LEVITES DID TO THEMSELVES BEFORE THEY COULD SERVE
4. HOW OLD A LEVITE WAS WHEN HE HAD TO STOP WORK
5. WERE GIVEN AS GIFTS TO AARON AND HIS SONS

make your choice

Have you ever stopped to thank God for the special people He has given you? *Lord I thank You for these people you've put in my life:*_____.

MONDAY NUMBERS 9:1-5, 15-23

TAKE THE challenge

check it out!

Aren't you glad God's in charge and you're not?

In verses 1-5 of our passage, we have one of those Old Testament "pictures" of the atonement that God commanded His people to celebrate. What was it? The _____ Did they obey? _____

How did God tell the Israelites when to move and when to camp (v. 17)? _____

Did they obey?_____ How does God speak to us today? _____ Do you obey?_____

make your Choice

God, when I read Your Word, help me to _____ _____ !

TUESDAY NUMBERS 10:1-13, 33-36

TAKE THE challenge

check it out!

Why is it always best to obey your leaders?

What did Moses and Aaron use instead of TV, radio, microphones, or cell phones to get messages to the people? _____ The sons of Aaron (the priests) were to blow these for different types of events. Cross out the event that is incorrect here: WHEN THEY WENT TO WAR OR INTO BATTLE / AT SPORTING EVENTS / WHEN THEY WERE CELEBRATING AND REJOICING (AT FEASTS, ETC.) / AT THE BEGINNING OF THE MONTH (NEW MOON) / OVER THEIR OFFERINGS.

How does God describe Himself at the end of verse 10? "__ _____ _____ _____ _____."

make your Choice

Some leaders in my life that God uses to give me direction are _____

I will be sure to stay tuned in and obedient to the direction God gives them for me!

167

WEDNESDAY NUMBERS 11:4-17

TAKE THE challenge

check it out!

Do you THANK or CRANK?

What did God give the people every day so that they could make bread cakes? _____

Were they happy and thankful that the Lord was providing food for them? _____ How did their complaining make God feel? _____

How did their complaining make Moses feel?

_____

make your Choice

Am I a complainer? I need to think about how my complaining affects my friends, my parents, my teachers, and others. Today, I have complained about_____

_____. Instead, I should thank God for _____.

THURSDAY NUMBERS 11:18-25, 31-33

TAKE THE challenge

check it out!

Do you know people who are always wishing for something else - never quite CONTENT with what they have? (Hint: Is it YOU?)

What did the people want? _____

- God said, "OK, I'll give you so much meat that you will _____!"

- What kind of creatures did He send them for meat? _____

_____ - After God sent the meat, He also sent a

_____, and many people died.

make your Choice

I want _____

so badly that I think about it all the time. *Lord, help me to be content with what You give me.*

168

FRIDAY NUMBERS 12:1-15

TAKE THE challenge

check it out!

Is God pleased when we are critical of the leaders He has chosen?

Who spoke against Moses? _____ and

_____ (They were his own brother

and sister!) How is Moses described in verse 3?

_____ How did God feel when

they spoke against His chosen leader? (v. 9) _____

How was Miriam punished for this? _____

make your Choice

Check the statements that are true about YOU.

☐ I respect and pray for my leaders and teachers.

☐ I complain about my teachers and mock them behind their backs.

☐ I criticize how my leaders do things.

☐ I want to treat my leaders with more respect, with God's help.

SATURDAY NUMBERS 13:1-3, 16-25

TAKE THE challenge

check it out!

Do you get excited when God asks you to do something new?

CANAAN
ESHCOL
FIGS
FORTY
FRUIT
GRAPES
LAND
PEOPLE
POMEGRANATES

```
F E Z H D Z H X U N C E
R S Z O U O T M I J I A
U H S Y P C Q P G X B B
I C T K T Y A R X D L X
P O M E G R A N A T E S
A L A S E P O T A Q H N
O Y G M E X Y F S A Q T
T I Y S E L P O E P N I
F L D T W Y V Q R J N U
Z U V T P B C A U T H R
U L A N D P E Q F F E F
```

make your Choice

Something new God wants me to do is _____

_____. I am AFRAID or EXCITED

(Circle one.) *Lord, help me to do this and trust YOU to help me!*

chart your course

MOSES - *the Political Leader (like the President or Prime Minister)*

AARON -*the Spiritual Leader or High Priest (like a national evangelist, like Dr. Billy Graham)*

CALEB AND JOSHUA - *the Military Leaders (like our national generals)*

SUNDAY   NUMBERS 13:26-14:5

TAKE THE challenge

What "perspective" do you have?

Who said this? ("The People" or "Caleb")

1. "The cities are too protected!"_____

2. "The people are too big!"_____

3. "We look like grasshoppers to them!"_____

4. "We can do it!"_____

5. "We should go back to Egypt!"_____

"Perspective" is how you look at or view a situation.

Caleb looked at the situation like God did!

check it out!

make your Choice

I want to trust God like Caleb did! Help me not be afraid to

_____

_____.

MONDAY NUMBERS 14:6-19

TAKE THE challenge

check it out!

Did you know. . . when our FEAR keeps us from obeying God, it means we don't really trust Him?

In which verse does it say two times "don't be afraid of the people" or "fear not"? verse _____ In verse 11, God says He has shown them many signs of His power and they still don't _____ Him.

make your Choice

What or who are you afraid of? _____

What do you worry about? _____

I BELIEVE / DON'T BELIEVE (circle one) that God has the power to help me with my fears. *God help me to trust you!*

TUESDAY NUMBERS 14:20-33

TAKE THE challenge

check it out!

How serious is complaining and unbelief to God?

What word did God use to describe those who complained against the Lord in verse 27? _____ Would they ever be allowed to live in the Promised Land?_____ (v. 30) How long did God say their children would wander in the wilderness because of their sins? _____ (v. 33) How did God describe Caleb in verse 24? _____

make your Choice

Today, I complained about _____.

God, the next time I'm tempted to complain, help me think of Caleb and be content with God's will for me.

WEDNESDAY NUMBERS 14:34-45

TAKE THE challenge

check it out!

How do you handle failure?

Down
1. THE TWO FAITHFUL SPIES-CALEB AND _____
3. WHAT THE MEN WHO BROUGHT THE BAD REPORT DIED OF

Across
2. NUMBER OF DAYS THE SPIES SEARCHED THE LAND (v. 34)
4. WHAT HAPPENED WHEN THEY WENT TO BATTLE WITHOUT THE LORD? "YE SHALL _____ BY THE SWORD"
5. WHAT THE PEOPLE DID WHEN THEY HEARD THE CONSEQUENCES OF THEIR SIN

make your Choice

When I fail I:
- [ ] Come up with my own plan to fix things
- [ ] Blame others
- [ ] Cry out to the Lord for help

THURSDAY NUMBERS 15:22-36

TAKE THE challenge

check it out!

It's all about your attitude!

Which verses talk about a sin that was committed accidentally, or unintentionally? _____ and _____ What could the priests do to atone for these sins? (vv. 24-26) _____

_____

Which verses talk about sins that were committed defiantly, in a way that despised God and His Word? _____ and _____ What was the consequence of that attitude of heart? ". . . that person (soul) shall be _____ _____: his _____ _____ be upon (on) h_____." (v. 31b)

make your Choice

God, I want to know how to _____

You. Show me when I sin so I can _____

_____

_____.

FRIDAY NUMBERS 17:1-11

TAKE THE challenge

check it out!

How does someone become a true leader?

What object did God ask the leader of each tribe to bring? _____ Was this object dead or alive? _____ The next day, what had Aaron's rod (or staff) done? Was it dead or alive? _____ What an illustration of God's life-giving power (RESURRECTION POWER!)! In verse 5, Aaron is described as "The man whom I (shall) _____."

make your Choice

God, I want to _____ the leaders whom You choose and empower to minister.

SATURDAY NUMBERS 20:1-12

TAKE THE challenge

check it out!

Do you ever get so frustrated with other people that you allow them to affect your attitude? Well, guess what? Even Moses got frustrated at times!

The people were_____ because there was no water. Moses and Aaron asked the Lord what they should do. Mark **T** if the statement is **TRUE**, or **F** if the statement is **FALSE**.

____ God promised water if Moses would speak to the rock.
____ Moses trusted God.
____ Moses called the people rebels.
____ Moses honored God and encouraged the people to look to Him for provision.
____ Moses struck the rock twice instead of speaking to it.
____ Moses was not allowed to enter the Promised Land.

make your Choice

Sometimes I am frustrated with bad attitudes at _____ _____. *Lord, help me not to use other people's attitudes to make excuses for my own bad attitudes and behavior.*

173

chart your course

SYMBOLS are important! Think of street signs. Letters and numbers are SYMBOLS. God uses SYMBOLS to remind us of important things. What do ✝ and 🐟 remind you of? Even in the Old Testament, God used SYMBOLS to teach His people about His character — from a snake on a pole . . . to special cities!

SUNDAY NUMBERS 20:23-21:9

TAKE THE challenge

Did you know that Jesus used stories from the Old Testament to illustrate the Gospel in the New Testament?

check it out!

Complaining again! How did God punish His children for complaining this time?_____ _____ What verse tells us that the people repented? _____ What provision did God make to allow them to be healed from the snake bites? _____ Look up John 3:14. What should the snake on the pole remind us of? _____ on the _____

make your Choice

Who am I looking to for my salvation?

_____

MONDAY NUMBERS 22:1-15

TAKE THE challenge

check it out!

How does God feel about those who try to hurt His people?

Down

2. THE MOABITES WERE _____ (pick one: ANGRY, HAPPY, AFRAID) OF ISRAEL BECAUSE THERE WERE SO MANY OF THEM.

4. BALAK ASKED BALAAM TO PUT A _____ ON THE CHILDREN OF ISRAEL.

Across

1. THE KING OF THE MOABITES

3. ISRAEL CAMPED IN THE PLAINS OF MOAB ACROSS FROM THIS CITY.

5. GOD TOLD HIM NOT TO CURSE THE PEOPLE BECAUSE THEY WERE_____ (v. 12).

make your Choice

Are you a child of God? Then you can feel safe! I know that nothing can hurt me because God calls me _____

_____.

TUESDAY NUMBERS 22:21-35

TAKE THE challenge

check it out!

Sometimes animals listen to God better than people!

Fill in the blanks to complete the account from this chapter: Balaam rode his _____ and went with the _____ but an _____ stood in the way. He could not see the _____, but his _____ could, and she turned off the road and Balaam _____ her. Then the donkey _____ Balaam's foot against a rock wall and she _____ down. Finally the donkey _____. Only then could Balaam _____ the angel.

make your Choice

Lord open my e_____ and e_____ to see and h_____ what You want me to do and help me to o_____ You.

175

TAKE THE challenge

check it out!

Why do we need leaders?

After Moses, who was to be the new leader?

_____ Verse 17 describes

what the people would be like if they DIDN'T have

a leader: "like _____ _____ _____ _____

_____" (How confusing would that be?)

Which verse says Joshua would have authority? [ ]

Which verses say Joshua would get decisions from God? [ ]

make your Choice

Some leaders in my life that I am thankful for are _____

_____. I think God may be asking

me to be a leader in my _____

_____.

TAKE THE challenge

check it out!

Do you ever want to take it easy while others are working?

Oh no! Not again! Years ago, the people didn't
want to go in and possess the land. Now which two
tribes were wanting to "stay put" and not cross the
Jordan? _____ and _____
Was Moses happy about this? _____ What phrase
in verse 6 tells us they were ready to rest when

there was still work to be done? "_____

_____" What was their attitude

doing to the rest of the Israelites? (v 7) _____ them.

make your Choice

Lord, give me the energy to be a _____ worker.

Help my enthusiasm to _____ others.

FRIDAY NUMBERS 32:16-31

TAKE THE challenge

check it out!

Is keeping a promise important?

What promise did the Gadites and Reubenites make in verse 18? _____

What does God call it if we DON'T keep our promise? (v 23) _____ What if no one ever finds out that you broke your promise (v 23)? "Be sure _____"

make your Choice

A promise I have made recently is _____
_____. Have I kept it? _____
What do I need to do? _____

SATURDAY NUMBERS 35:9-25

TAKE THE challenge

check it out!

It's good to have a safe place.

This is another one of those "pictures" or "symbols" of God's mercy in the Old Testament. What were these special cities to be called? Cities of _____
_____ Were they for the protection of someone who killed someone on purpose? _____
(v 16-21) Were they for the protection of someone who killed someone accidentally? _____ (v 11 & 15)

make your Choice

Look at Psalms 46:1 to see what God is called: "Our _____
_____ and Strength" *Thank you, God, for being my _____
_____ (my safe place) even when I sin.*

177

chart your course

When you think of FREEDOM in America, you might think of United States documents like The Emancipation Proclamation and The Bill of Rights. This letter of Paul's lays the groundwork for SPIRITUAL FREEDOM: Liberty in Christ! Along with Romans and Hebrews, it has been called The Bill of Rights of the Christian Life!

SUNDAY GALATIANS 1:1-9

TAKE THE challenge

How would you define the Gospel?

check it out!

Before Paul shares his concerns about their accepting a gospel that was not "the real thing," he gives them "the real thing" in verse four. Write it out below the cross.

JESUS CHRIST, "Who

_____

_____ **Father."**

make your Choice

What did Jesus do on the cross for me? _____

_____

MONDAY GALATIANS 1:10-17

TAKE THE challenge

check it out!

How did Jesus change your life when you trusted Him as Savior?

Paul wanted these confused Galatian believers to understand the truth of the Gospel ("Good News"). He says in verses 11 and 12 that the Gospel he preached:

1) Was not _____

2) Was not received from _____

3) It was not _____ to him.

4) It came by the _____ of _____ _____

Name three locations Paul mentions in his personal testimony:

_____, _____ and _____

make your Choice

Look at verse 10. Paul asks us a very important question. Am I trying to please _____ or _____?

I cannot be a true servant of _____ if I only care about pleasing people!

TUESDAY GALATIANS 1:18-24

TAKE THE challenge

check it out!

When you share your testimony of how you came to know Christ, do you tell about the people that shared Christ with you?

Two people who had helped Paul in his new faith were _____ and _____, the _____ _____'s brother. WOW! Imagine being taught by Jesus Christ's own brother! Unscramble the three locations Paul visited in his early Christian life.

MEERLASUJ __ __ __ __ __ __ __ __ __ __

LAICCII __ __ __ __ __ __ __

RAISY __ __ __ __ __

make your Choice

What was the biggest thing that changed in my life when I became a Christian? _____

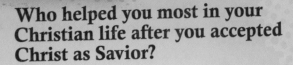

TAKE THE challenge

check it out!

Who helped you most in your Christian life after you accepted Christ as Savior?

The men who helped Paul grow in his Christian faith did much of their instruction in private since he was a well-known public figure. The two men mentioned are _____ and _____.

But there were also some Christian brothers who were trying to force those who were free in Christ to live by old Jewish laws.

make your Choice

Write a thank you letter to someone who has helped or taught you in your Christian life! I praise God for _____

_____.

THURSDAY GALATIANS 2:7-14

TAKE THE challenge

Do you ever act one way with one person and another way with someone else?

Write down four very important disciples Paul writes about in these verses:

_____   _____

_____   _____

check it out!

These men all met for a "conference" and agreed that Paul should go to evangelize the _____ and they should go to the _____ (v. 9). Paul confronted _____ about acting one way with James and another way with the Jewish believers.

make your Choice

A "hypocrite" is someone who acts one way with some people and a whole different way with others. How have I acted like a hypocrite?

FRIDAY GALATIANS 2:15-21

TAKE THE challenge

check it out!

What do you think it means to be "justified"?

As you read these verses, what two words stand out as the most important? j _____ and f _____ Being justified means that before God I am "JUST as if I had never sinned" because I am forgiven of all my _____. Verses 15-16 tell us we can only be justified by _____ in _____ and not by the _____.

make your Choice

"Write out verse 20 and see if you can memorize it!

_____

_____

_____ for me." Galatians 2:20

SATURDAY GALATIANS 3:1-9

TAKE THE challenge

check it out!

What does a person need to do to be saved for eternity?

What does Paul call the Galatian Christians? "O _____ Galatians!" He asks them, "Who has _____ you?" He was concerned that they had been fooled by false teaching to think they had to add works to their faith in order to be saved. Whom did he use as an Old Testament example of saving faith? _____ He says that this man _____ God and it was _____ to him for _____.

make your Choice

As one who has put my faith in God for salvation, whom am I "blessed with" according to verse 9?

chart your course

DID YOU KNOW THAT . . .

This is the only letter of Paul addressed to multiple churches?

During Paul's 2nd missionary journey he was delayed in Galatia by sickness?

SUNDAY GALATIANS 3:10-16

TAKE THE challenge

Whom do you know that is perfect – has kept the whole law of God without ever making a mistake?

check it out!

Paul reminds the confused Galatian believers that anyone who relies on obeying all of God's law for salvation is really "under the (a) _____." Since no one can obey it perfectly, they would have no hope of salvation. Then Paul quotes a famous Old Testament Scripture, Habakkuk 2:4, "The _____ shall _____ by _____." Only _____ can redeem us "from the _____ of the _____."

make your Choice

My salvation is based totally on what _____ did, not anything _____ did. Whom can I share Christ with today? _____

MONDAY GALATIANS 3:17-22

TAKE THE challenge

check it out!

Do you look in the mirror each morning when you get ready for school?

Verses 17-21 share how the Law or commandments of God are like a mirror of the heart, showing us our sin so we can come to Christ for salvation. Verse 22 tells us that all people in the world are under the curse or bondage of __ __ __ so that God's promise of salvation by (through) _____ in _____ _____ would be available to all who _____.

make your choice

What was I like before Jesus saved me from sin? _____
_____ Do I know someone who doesn't know Jesus as Savior? Write their name here and pray for them this week: _____

TUESDAY GALATIANS 3:23-29

TAKE THE challenge

check it out!

Do I think some kinds of people are better than others?

We are all the _____ of _____ through faith in Jesus Christ. As children of God, we are all equally important in God's sight. Draw lines between the things that match:

JEW •   • FREE

SLAVE/BOND •   • IN CHRIST JESUS

MALE •   • GREEK

ALL ONE •   • FEMALE

make your choice

Verse 29b tells me I am one of God's and Abraham's
"_____ according to the _____."
What have I inherited from Jesus?

183

WEDNESDAY GALATIANS 4:1-7

TAKE THE challenge

How important is "time" to you? Do you wear a watch?

check it out!

God's timing is perfect! At just the perfect time in the world's history, God _____ His _____, _____ of a _____, _____ under the _____, so that He could r_____ those who were under the _____. Because of God's gift of redemption in Christ, I went from a s_____ to a _____ to an _____ of promise!

make your Choice

Verse 6 tells me that as God's child, I can call Him
"_____" or "Daddy"!
When I pray to God, do I picture Him as my DADDY? YES / NO

THURSDAY GALATIANS 4:8-18

TAKE THE challenge

When was the last time you were sick with the flu or a cold?

check it out!

Verse 13 tells us that it was through his _____ _____ that he had first preached to the Galatians. Even though his being sick had been hard for them, they had received or welcomed him as an "_____ of God" and as Jesus _____ Himself! Paul wanted them to accept the _____ (v. 16) he was now telling them.

make your Choice

Is there someone I know who is sick and in need of encouragement? _____
_____

184

FRIDAY GALATIANS 4:19-26

check it out!

Have you ever been so burdened for a friend or family member to come to know Christ that it hurt?

Paul was so concerned for the Galatians to know and grow in Christ that he says it felt like (circle one) drowning ~ childbirth pains ~ being crucified. Unscramble the Old Testament names Paul refers to in explaining freedom in Christ:

NASII __ __ __ __ __ (A MOUNTAIN)

RGAAH __ __ __ __ __ (A WOMAN)

RHAAMAB __ __ __ __ __ __ __ (A MAN)

make your Choice

What unsaved person do I care enough about to pray for everyday? _____

_____

SATURDAY GALATIANS 4:27-5:1

TAKE THE challenge

check it out!

How would you define "FREEDOM" to someone?

After finishing his comparison of Abraham's sons, he says that we, just like Isaac, are "_____ of _____" (v. 28). Copy verse 1 of chapter 5 on the Freedom Banner below:

" _____
_____
_____ ."

Galatians 5:1

make your Choice

What sometimes keeps me from enjoying my freedom in Christ?

_____

_____

chart your course

Have you noticed all the CONTRASTING things the book of Galatians addresses?

CONDEMNATION **VS.** justification

LAW **VS.** grace

WORKS **VS.** faith

BONDAGE **VS.** freedom

LOST IN ADAM **VS.** saved in christ

SUNDAY — GALATIANS 5:2-6

TAKE THE challenge

Do you ever try to live a good Christian life in your own strength?

check it out!

To understand this passage you must know what "circumcision" means. It was a Jewish bodily ritual that was done to show separation from the world unto God alone. But in verse 6, Paul says that in Christ neither c_____ or u_____ has any value. The only thing that really counts is f_____ working (expressing itself) by l_____.

make your Choice

There is a difference in my working FOR God and letting God work THROUGH me. What part of the Christian life do I try to do on my own instead of by GOD's strength? _____

_____

MONDAY GALATIANS 5:7-15

TAKE THE challenge

check it out!

When was the last time you said ugly or unkind words to someone?

After explaining the whole issue about the false teaching that had affected them, Paul reminded the Galatian believers that the entire law could be summed up in one single command: "_____ _____."

Then he told them that they would destroy or consume each other if they continued to _____ and _____ each other.

make your Choice

How do I "bite and devour" others when I am angry or in a bad mood? _____

How does this dishonor God's command to LOVE? _____ _____

TUESDAY GALATIANS 5:16-21

TAKE THE challenge

check it out!

Do you ever feel like there is a fight going on inside you?

This is a passage of contrasts. In verses 16-18, Paul contrasts living (or walking) by the _____ with the sinful nature (flesh). In the word puzzle below, find at least six works, acts or deeds of "the flesh" or sinful nature.

A	N	D	U	I	M	M	O	R	A	L	I	T	Y	A
E	S	A	L	H	A	T	R	E	D	A	M	P	A	D
U	T	G	K	J	L	D	A	I	U	G	P	O	E	I
V	R	A	N	S	W	A	Q	S	L	J	U	Y	N	S
W	I	T	C	H	C	R	A	F	T	S	R	I	V	C
H	F	A	J	S	I	D	O	P	E	A	I	T	Y	O
E	E	Z	B	Q	A	F	A	M	R	H	T	A	L	R
J	G	I	D	O	L	A	T	R	Y	A	Y	T	Y	D
H	A	S	X	D	R	U	N	K	E	N	N	E	S	S

make your Choice

I will choose to walk or live in the _____,

not in the _____.

187

WEDNESDAY GALATIANS 5:22-26

TAKE THE challenge

check it out!

If you could be a fruit tree, what kind of tree would you like to be?

Write the names of "the fruit of the spirit" under each piece of fruit.

_____

_____

_____

_____   _____   _____

make your Choice

What are three kinds of spiritual fruit that I need to let God's Spirit produce in MY life? _____, _____, and _____ Which one do I struggle with most? (Circle it.)

THURSDAY GALATIANS 6:1-5

TAKE THE challenge

check it out!

Do you have a friend who is a Christian, but may be going away from God or struggling in his faith?

Here are some wonderful tips for helping other struggling believers: 1) If they are _____ in a _____, try to _____ them meekly and gently. 2) Watch (consider) _____, though, to make sure you are not about to fall into the same sin or temptation. 3) Help _____ each other's burdens. 4) Have a **PROUD/ HUMBLE** (circle one) attitude. 5) Evaluate your own spiritual life to make sure you are on track!

make your Choice

With what struggling Christian friend will I apply the above tips this week? _____

FRIDAY GALATIANS 6:6-10

TAKE THE challenge

check it out!

When was the last time you planted something and watched it grow?

Paul uses a gardening illustration to share with us the laws of the harvest in these verses:

LAWS OF THE HARVEST

Match the correct answers;

_____ 1. What you sow

_____ 2. Sow to the flesh (sinful nature)

_____ 3. Sow to the Spirit

_____ 4. Reap a harvest

A. Reap eternal life
B. In the proper season (due time)
C. You will reap
D. Reap destruction or corruption

make your Choice

Write down one way you are sowing to the flesh, then ask God's forgiveness: _____

Now write down one way you are (or will be) sowing to the SPIRIT: _____

SATURDAY GALATIANS 6:11-18

TAKE THE challenge

check it out!

What do you like to brag or boast about most?

Paul says the reason some wrong teachers had been pushing circumcision was that they wanted to outwardly impress certain people in order to avoid persecution. But look at verses 14 and 15! He says he never wants to _____, except (save) in the _____ of our _____ _____ _____, through (by) whom the _____ has been _____ to me, and I to the _____. He goes on to add that c_____ or u_____ is not the important thing, but rather "a _____ _____."

make your Choice

Am I a new creature (creation) in Christ? Yes/No Then I should be bragging or boasting only about what? _____

_____

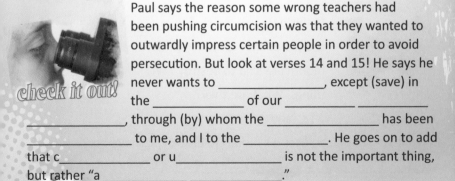

chart your course

"Proverbs" are big truths contained in little verses. How cool is that? You'll see the tiny word **"BUT"** many times in a number of contrasting statements like, "When pride cometh, then cometh shame: **BUT** with the lowly is wisdom."

SUNDAY PROVERBS 11:1-11

TAKE THE challenge

How important are my words?

check it out!

In this passage, the mouth or the words that come out of the mouth are said to destroy TWO things. What are they?

_____ and _____

What kind of person uses his mouth to destroy his neighbor?

_____

make your Choice

Lord, help me not to say anything today that will hurt feelings or reputations. I need to apologize to _____ for something I have said about or to him or her.

TAKE THE challenge

Do you have to say everything you know?

check it out!

Fill in the verse number for these principles:

☐ Be kind.

☐ Don't gossip.

☐ Righteousness will be rewarded.

☐ Wickedness will be punished.

☐ It's not smart to talk badly about your neighbor.

make your Choice

I will circle the principle above that I most need God's help with today.

TUESDAY PROVERBS 11:22-31

TAKE THE challenge

How do you feel about the things God has blessed you with?

check it out!

God paints a word picture in verses 24 and 25 of the person who loves to share. What words does he use? _____Does this person ever run out of what he needs?_____

What happens to the person who trusts in his riches? _____ "BUT the righteous _____ "

make your Choice

God, help me to trust _____ to meet my needs and to always share what You give me with others. I want to hold onto Your blessings loosely, with open hands!

191

TAKE THE challenge

Do you like to be punished? (Please say NO!)

check it out!

What? Are you crazy? Does verse one really SAY that?

Write out verse one here: "_____

_____

_____

_____

_____."

make your Choice

Lord, help me to appreciate and be thankful for the correction and discipline you send into my life to make me a better person. Sometimes that discipline comes through my

_____ *or* _____.

TAKE THE challenge

How good are you at taking advice?

check it out!

What does this passage call the person who thinks

his way is the only right way? _____

How does it describe the person who listens to

advice? _____

make your Choice

Am I a TEACHABLE person? _____ How do I respond when I

am corrected or given advice? _____

_____

_____

FRIDAY PROVERBS 12:20-28

TAKE THE challenge

check it out!

GUESS WHAT?
Your "Quality of Life" is determined by how you live!

ACROSS
3. What is in the way of righteousness?
4. What those who work hard will do (v.24).

DOWN
1. What is in the hearts of those who plan evil
2. Where the fool's foolishness comes from (v.23b).
5. What the Lord detests: _____ lips

make your choice

Lord, I believe that You desire for me to have more _____
_____ and less
_____ in my life today.

Teach me to promote those qualities that You want in my life.

SATURDAY PROVERBS 13:1-13

TAKE THE challenge

check it out!

When you want something, what do you do?

Look at verse 4. What kind of person wants something, but doesn't get it? _____
(Do you need to look that word up in the dictionary?)
Verse 4 also says that a diligent person (hard worker) has his desires satisfied. Verse 11 talks about doing what with money? (Check all that apply.)

- ☐ Winning it in the lottery
- ☐ Working for it
- ☐ Spending it
- ☐ Saving it

make your choice

I would really like to have_____.
I believe God wants me to _____
in order to get it.

193

chart your course

The Principle Theme of the Book of Proverbs is WISDOM. The words WISE and WISDOM occur more than 100 times in this book and the word UNDERSTANDING occurs more than 50 times. Make slash marks here each time you see any word that comes from WISE or WISDOM as you study the Proverbs this week:

WISE

TOTAL: _____

SUNDAY PROVERBS 13:14-25

TAKE THE challenge

check it out!

Does it really matter who you hang out with?

What happens if you hang out with wise people? _____
_____
_____

Why is it not safe to hang out with fools?

_____

make your Choice

The people that I spend most of my time with (check one):
_____ Help me learn more about the Lord.
_____ Draw my mind away from the things of the Lord.

TAKE THE challenge

So who can get wisdom and how can you get it?

check it out!

First, read through the passage and mark every time you see the words wise, wisdom, knowledge, or understand (-eth or -ing). Finished with that? How many did you count today? _____ Now focus on verse 6. Who can't get wisdom? _____

Why?_____ (It's because of his attitude.)

make your Choice

Lord, give me a teachable attitude, not the attitude of one who mocks Your kind of wisdom.

TAKE THE challenge

Do you believe everything you hear or see?

check it out!

The word "prudent" means "marked by skill, wisdom, or good judgment." In which two verses in today's passage do you find the word "prudent" or "sensible"?

☐ and ☐ Verse 15 says that a "simple" man (opposite of prudent) believes anything.

What does a prudent man do? (Check both verses in which you found that word.) _____

make your Choice

Before I believe something I hear on TV, in my classroom, or on the internet, I will _____

_____

_____.

TAKE THE challenge

Can our attitude affect our health?

check it out!

Draw lines to match the phrases from today's passage.

Treats poor badly •   • **Great understanding**

Envy (passion) •   • **Rottenness of bones**

Righteous •   • **Has hope even in death**

Slow to wrath (patient) •   • **Shows contempt for their Maker**

make your Choice

God, help me to be a patient, content person because I trust you. I ask You to help me have a _____ attitude today.

TAKE THE challenge

Can HOW we speak affect how our words are received?

check it out!

Verse 1 - What kind of words turn away wrath?

_____

What kind of words stir up wrath? _____

_____

Which verses describe a wise tongue? _____

Which verse describes a wholesome or healing

tongue? _____

make your Choice

Dear Lord, today, I'm going to try speaking _____ and _____ when I am talking to others, even to those I don't usually get along with. Please help me.

196

FRIDAY PROVERBS 15:12-22

check it out!

Have you ever noticed? . . . The smartest people are always trying to learn more!

Verse 12 - What does the Bible call someone who

doesn't want to learn_____?

Verse 14 - _____ seeks knowledge

Verse 22 - What is needed for plans to succeed?

_____

make your Choice

I need to learn more about _____.

I need to be more open to _____'s

(person's name) teaching in my life.

SATURDAY PROVERBS 15:23-33

TAKE THE challenge

THINK . . . about the words coming out of your mouth and the look on your face!

check it out!

Verse 28 - What word tells us to think before we

answer? _____

Verse 30 - What can the cheerful look on our face do to someone

else's heart? _____

_____

make your Choice

When I walk into _____

(place) I will make a conscious effort to smile at _____

_____(person) to communicate God's love today. 197

chart your course

Write out the name on the line below of the city that is circled on the map. This city was home to the new church Paul was writing this letter to.

_____

SUNDAY   1 THESSALONIANS 1:1-5

TAKE THE challenge

If someone were writing about you, what would he or she remember about you?

check it out!

There are many "threes" in this passage.
Three men writing to the Thessalonian believers:
1) _____, 2) _____,
3) _____. Three members of the
Trinity (God's names): (1) God the _____
2) The Lord _____ 3) The _____ _____ (v. 5).
Three good things Paul remembered about these believers (v. 3):
1) _____ 2) _____
3) _____

make your Choice

Who are three people I thank God for today?

_____

_____

_____

MONDAY 1 THESSALONIANS 1:6-10

TAKE THE challenge

Whom do you look up to as an example of Christianity?

check it out!

These new believers had become followers or imitators of whom? (Circle two.) Paul and his CO-WORKERS / THE LORD / THEIR SCHOOL TEACHERS

How did they receive or welcome the message of God's Word? With _____ in the Holy _____! Unscramble the places where God's Word was spread by the Thessalonian believers: HAACIA __ __ __ __ __ __ DAMECIONA __ __ __ __ __ __ __ __ __ and in YEEVR __ __ __ __ __ place!

make your Choice

Who imitates me or follows MY example?? _____
_____
Are my actions, attitudes, and words worth imitating? YES / NO

TUESDAY 1 THESSALONIANS 2:1-8

TAKE THE challenge

Who in this world do you most want to impress or please?

check it out!

What are three things that did NOT come or spring from Paul's message to these believers (v. 3)? NOT from (of) _____ or _____ or _____. Paul said that they spoke NOT to please _____ but _____ "Who _____ our _____ (v. 4)."

make your Choice

Whom should I seek to please as I live my life as a Christian?
_____

199

WEDNESDAY 1 THESSALONIANS 2:9-13

TAKE THE challenge

check it out!

What kind of witness are you to others?

Paul says they labored _____ and _____ in order to get the gospel message to them. He said both God and the Thessalonian believers were witnesses to how _____ , _____ , and _____ they had acted toward the believers (v. 10). They had ministered God's Word to these young believers as a _____ does to his _____ .

make your Choice

Look at verse 12. What would it look like for me to live a life worthy of God and His kingdom? _____
_____
_____

THURSDAY 1 THESSALONIANS 2:14-20

TAKE THE challenge

Has anyone ever tried to stop you from living for Jesus?

check it out!

Paul had been persecuted and driven out by the _____ (v. 14) and stopped many times from coming to Thessalonica by _____ (v. 18). But he says these growing believers are his

_____ , _____ , and _____ of rejoicing or delight. They made all the hardships worth it!

make your Choice

Write the name of one person I've helped or ministered to in some way. _____

How does this make me feel? _____

FRIDAY 1 THESSALONIANS 3:1-5

TAKE THE challenge

check it out!

What kind of trial or hardship have you faced lately?

Whom did Paul send to the Thessalonians in their trials? _____ Paul calls him "our _____ and (God's) _____ in the _____ of Christ. He was sent to do what two things? To _____ and to _____ them in their faith.

make your Choice

How could I strengthen or encourage someone in his or her faith today? _____

_____

_____

SATURDAY 1 THESSALONIANS 3:6-13

TAKE THE challenge

check it out!

When was the last time you got a report card from school?

Timothy gave the Thessalonian believers an A+ in which areas listed below:

THESSALONIAN REPORT CARD		MY REPORT CARD
_____	Their faith	_____
_____	Their love (charity)	_____
_____	Good memories of Paul	_____
_____	Standing firm (fast) in the Lord	_____
_____	Giving us joy before God	_____

(v.10) Paul prayed fervently for them n_____ and d_____ - (v.12-13) that their _____ for others would increase and their hearts would be established (strengthened) in _____ _____ before God.

make your Choice

Put an X by the area above in which I would have received a bad grade.. How do I need to improve in this area? _____

_____

chart your course

Paul wrote this letter while he was in Corinth. Thessalonica was a busy seaport city located at the junction of two main roads. It was the largest city in Macedonia (not Greece). Paul had only ministered here for a few short weeks during his second missionary journey.

SUNDAY 1 THESSALONIANS 4:1-8

TAKE THE challenge

Who created sex? Who, then, do you think has the best plan for it?

check it out!

This whole passage is about God's plan for sexual purity before marriage. God designed sex to be between one _____ and one _____ for _____. (Choose from these words to complete the above: woman, awhile, angel, man, life) According to verse 3, what is God's will for each of us? _____ _____. This means we are to keep our bodies pure for the mate GOD has for us one day and to never commit sexual acts outside of marriage!

make your Choice

Write out your own commitment to God here concerning sexual purity: I commit to _____ _____

202

MONDAY 1 THESSALONIANS 4:9-12

TAKE THE challenge

Do you know what a "work ethic" is? Ask your dad or mom!

check it out!

Part of being able to work together is having more brotherly l_____ toward one another. Paul was coaching these believers to be productive employees or workers. He wanted them to make it their goal (study, ambition) to do three things at work: 1) To be _____ or lead a _____ life. 2) Mind (do / attend) your own _____ 3) _____ with your own _____ .

make your Choice

Verse 12 states that if I have a godly work ethic, I will win the respect of others who watch me. What kind of worker am I?

_____

_____

TUESDAY 1 THESSALONIANS 4:13-18

TAKE THE challenge

Are you ready for Jesus to come back for you today?

Put the following events (that could happen at any time) in order, numbering them from 1–7.

___ The Lord Himself will descend from Heaven.

___ The dead in Christ will go up.

___ He'll descend with a SHOUT or loud command.

___ We'll be with the LORD forever!

___ Christians who are still alive will be caught up with Jesus.

___ The voice of the archangel will be heard.

make your Choice

How can I (as verse 18 tells me) ENCOURAGE others with these truths? _____

_____

WEDNESDAY · 1 THESSALONIANS 5:1-8

TAKE THE challenge

check it out!

Have you ever had a thief break into your home? Did he let you know what time he'd break in?

1. What will come like "a thief in the night"?

_____ ___ ____ _____

2. What will people be saying when it happens (v. 3)?

" _____and _____ "

3. As believers, we are all _____ of the

_____ and of the _____.

make your Choice

According to this passage, in order to be ready (prepared) for

Jesus' surprise coming, I need to be (check them): ☐ lazy

☐ helpful   ☐ having fun   ☐ asleep   ☐ loving

☐ self-controlled   ☐ sober-minded   ☐ watchful   ☐ hopeful

THURSDAY · 2 THESSALONIANS 5:9-15

TAKE THE challenge

check it out!

Who has encouraged or helped you spiritually during the last week?

Match the following:

_____ 1. God appointed us

_____ 2. Comfort and encourage

_____ 3. Those who work with you and are over you

_____ 4. Be at or live in

_____ 5. Those who are unruly or idle

_____ 6. Be patient

A. And build up and edify

B. Warn them

C. With all (everyone)

D. To salvation

E Respect, know, esteem highly

F Peace with each other

make your Choice

Look at verses 14 through 15. Which one of these commands do I

especially need to work on? Write it here: _____

_____

FRIDAY 1 THESSALONIANS 5:16-22

TAKE THE challenge

check it out!

How do you feel about tests? Do you do well on them?

There are at least eight Christian commands here.
Write five of them on the lines below:

(1) _____

(2) _____

(3) _____

(4) _____

(5) _____

make your Choice

Verse 21 tells me to test, evaluate, or examine everything I do in light of what is good. What in my life is questionable by God's standards? _____

What do I need to DO about it? _____

SATURDAY 1 THESSALONIANS 5:23-28

TAKE THE challenge

check it out!

Do you know what "sanctify" means?

Verse 23 tells us that God Himself – the God of _____ - will S_____ us, so we can be preserved (kept) _____ until He comes. In the three-part circle, label the areas of our lives that He wants to sanctify or set apart in His holiness. Find them in verse 23.

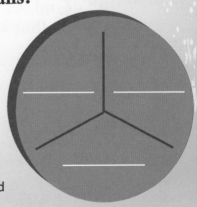

make your Choice

Look at verse 24 and put "ME" in place of the "you" in this verse. Jesus "who calls (calleth) _____ is faithful, and He will do it (bring it to pass)! " Who can I count on to sanctify me? _____

205

chart your course

Let's do some detective work! Find out who really wrote this second letter to the Thessalonian believers by checking out chapter 1, verse 1 and chapter 3, verse 17. Underline the helpers and circle the main writer of this letter:

SILAS
TIMOTHY
SILVANUS
TIMOTHEUS
PAUL

SUNDAY

2 THESSALONIANS 1:1-5

TAKE THE challenge

If someone were to thank God for you, what would he be thankful for?

check it out!

For what two things did Paul and his companions in ministry always thank God?

(1) _____

(2) _____

What two things did they brag to the others churches about (v. 4)?

"Your _____ and _____ "

make your Choice

What could my teacher, pastor, or club leader be thankful for or brag about concerning ME? _____

_____

MONDAY 2 THESSALONIANS 1:6-12

TAKE THE challenge

check it out!

Have you ever really thought about what will happen to those who are not Christians?

Whom will God punish with fire, according to verses 7 and 8? _____

_____

Verse 9 tells us that they will be punished with

e_____ d_____ from

the p_____ of the LORD.

make your Choice

What does God want ME to do to keep unbelievers from suffering

forever in Hell? _____

_____

TUESDAY 2 THESSALONIANS 2:1-5

TAKE THE challenge

check it out!

What do you think the evil antichrist will look like?

Circle the things from this passage that describe the antichrist ("son of perdition," "man of lawlessness"):

Doomed to destruction   **Deceptive**

Opposes God   **Loves Jesus**

Exalts God   **Acts like he is God**

Exalts himself over God   **Rebellious**

make your Choice

How can I keep from being deceived by ungodly people? _____

_____

_____

WEDNESDAY 2 THESSALONIANS 2:6-12

TAKE THE challenge

Do you ever hear others use the word "damn" when they are angry? What does this word really mean?

check it out!

Verses 6 and 7 tell us that God is holding back the Wicked or Lawless One until HE chooses to rid the world of him and his evil. Verse 8 says that when he is _____, the Lord Jesus will _____ him with the _____ of His mouth and destroy or stop him by the _____ of His coming. This satanic miracle-worker is the antichrist. We should never use the word "damn" in a casual way since it is God's eternal judgment on someone.

make your Choice

Are there sinful things that Satan has tricked me into enjoying or participating in? What are they? _____

_____

_____

THURSDAY 2 THESSALONIANS 2:13-17

TAKE THE challenge

Has anyone ever prayed a special blessing over you and your life?

check it out!

Paul, Silas, and Timothy were so thankful for these believers because God had appointed (chosen) them to salvation through two things:

(1) Sanctification of (by) God's _____

(2) _____ of (in) the truth (of the Gospel) In verse 15, Paul told them to _____ in the truths of the Word they had been taught.

make your Choice

Write out the beautiful blessing Paul prayed over the Thessalonian believers in vv. 16 and 17and claim it for yourself today! "_____

_____

_____"

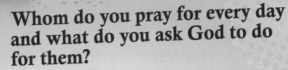
TAKE THE challenge

check it out!

Whom do you pray for every day and what do you ask God to do for them?

Paul asks the Thessalonians to pray two things for him and tells them two things HE prays for THEM. Can you find these requests in the passage? PRAY FOR PAUL:

(1) (v. 1) _____

(2) (v. 2) _____

PAUL PRAYS FOR THE THESSALONIANS: (1) That the faithful LORD will _____ and _____ you from evil or the evil one (v. 3). (2) "May the LORD _____ your _____" into God's love and patient waiting for Christ's return (v. 5).

make your Choice

What missionary or pastor can you pray the first two prayers for today? _____

Pray for them right now.

_____

SATURDAY 2 THESSALONIANS 3:6-18

TAKE THE challenge

Do you have a good work ethic? A "work ethic" means how you feel about working hard and doing your best.

check it out!

In verses 6-15, Paul addresses a big problem in the Thessalonian church: There were those who didn't want to (circle the correct one) eat - have fun - work. Complete the two good commands or rules Paul gives in verses 10b and 13 about working: (1) If anyone is not willing to _____, he shouldn't _____. (2) _____ _____. Finally, in verse 16, Paul asks God to bless these believers with His p_____: "The _____ be _____ _____ _____."

make your Choice

Check the one that best describes me: [ ] I am a hard worker and always try to do my very best. [ ] I work when I have to in order to get by. [ ] I hate to work and avoid it as much as I can.

chart your course

This letter – written by Paul from his house prison in Rome – was written to the church group in Colosse – an important trade city in what is now Turkey.

SUNDAY COLOSSIANS 1:1-8

TAKE THE challenge

What might someone hear about you that would cause them to thank God for you?

LETTER TO COLOSSIAN BELIEVERS

FROM: _____ and _____
TO: The _____ and _____
brothers (brethren) in _____ who
are at _____.

THANKFUL IN OUR PRAYERS FOR (check them):

[ ] Your faith in Christ
[ ] You have heard the truth of the Gospel.
[ ] You go to church every Sunday.
[ ] Your hope of Heaven
[ ] You learned from Epaphras.
[ ] Your love for the saints
[ ] The Gospel is bearing (bringing forth) fruit

check it out!

make your Choice

Write a thank you note to a Christian who has been a blessing to you, and get it to him.

MONDAY COLOSSIANS 1:9-14

TAKE THE challenge

Whom do you know that prays for you on a regular basis?

check it out!

Paul and Timothy never stopped _____ for the Colossian believers. Write down at least two things they were praying for in the Colossians' lives.

(1) _____

(2)_____

At the end of their prayer, they thanked God the Father for delivering them (us) from the _____ of _____ and bringing them (us) into the kingdom of His Son, In Whom they had r_____ (through Christ's blood) even the f_____ of sins.

make your Choice

Write down two important things I will pray faithfully for someone I love. (1) _____

(2) _____

TUESDAY COLOSSIANS 1:15-19

TAKE THE challenge

Have you ever wondered what would happen if God, the Creator, simply let go of the atoms He holds together?

check it out!

Match the things about Jesus (from the passage) by drawing lines between:

Jesus is the image of	*And the invisible*
He created things in	*Or dominions, or principalities, or rulers (powers)*
He created the visible	*By Him and for Him*
He created thrones	*Of the body – the church*
All things were created	*Heaven and on earth*
He is the head	The invisible God

make your Choice

If Jesus is **IN** all and **OVER** all, how can I make sure He has first place in MY life?

211

WEDNESDAY COLOSSIANS 1:20-23

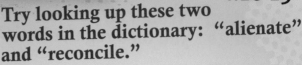

TAKE THE challenge

check it out!

Try looking up these two words in the dictionary: "alienate" and "reconcile."

Use the words here to complete the GOSPEL acrostic below: LIFE BLOOD CROSS RECONCILED PEACE HOLINESS

G od _____ us to Himself by Jesus'
O wn _____
S hed on the _____. Salvation means
P _____ with God,
E verlasting _____ in Heaven
L iving in Christ's _____.

make your Choice

The first two letters of GOSPEL spell "_____". To whom will I GO to share the Gospel with this week? _____
_____

THURSDAY COLOSSIANS 1:24-29

TAKE THE challenge

check it out!

Do you like mysteries? Do you keep secrets well?

As believers, Paul says we understand a

m_____ that many godly

people through the ages have not

known (v. 26). Verse 27 tells us the key

to this glorious mystery: "_____

in _____, the _____

of _____."

make your Choice

What kind of glory do I have to look forward to because Jesus is inside me? _____
_____

212

FRIDAY COLOSSIANS 2:1-7

TAKE THE challenge

check it out!

Do you have a special treasure box where you keep all your souvenirs and mementos?

Verse 3 reminds us of a wonderful truth: In Jesus Christ are hidden "all the _____ of _____ and _____." Look at verses 6-7 and number the following in the right order:

____ Receive Jesus as Lord.   ____ Be rooted and built up in Him.
____ Continue to walk (live) in Him.   ____ Abound or overflow with thankfulness. ____ Be stablished (strengthened) in the faith.

make your Choice

Circle one of the five things above that I will work on with God's help.

SATURDAY COLOSSIANS 2:8-15

TAKE THE challenge

check it out!

What does Jesus' death have to do with my victory as a Christian?

What did Jesus' death do, according to these verses? Circle them below:

Helps you get more friends   Victory over death

Forgave all sins   Cancelled out the old rules, regulations, and ordinances

Spoiled or disarmed principalities, rulers, authorities, and powers   Triumphed over all!

Makes you wealthy

make your Choice

What do others see in my life that shows them I'm a victorious Christian?

213

chart your course

DID YOU KNOW . . .

Epaphras took the Gospel message to Colosse?

The church at Colosse was made up of Gentiles, not Jews?

Philemon was a member of this church family?

False teachers had come in and were teaching the people to worship angels.

SUNDAY COLOSSIANS 2:16-23

TAKE THE challenge

check it out!

Did you know that every single year hundreds of new religions and cults are started?

Many of the things Paul addresses in this passage have to do with the focuses of false teachings and occult religions that false teachers were introducing in this young church. What are the three kinds of rules, ordinances or decrees that false religions often demand (v. 21)? Write them on these signs.

make your Choice

Who or what will I choose to worship and trust? (Circle one.)

Religious rules   Angels   Magic   Jesus

MONDAY COLOSSIANS 3:1-7

TAKE THE challenge

check it out!

What kinds of things do you think about in a day?

What fleshly sins do we need to "mortify" or put to death in order to make Jesus #1 in our lives? Circle all you see in the word puzzle. (No hints this time!)

T	C	O	V	E	T	O	U	S	N	E	S	S	D
I	M	M	O	R	A	L	I	T	Y	H	H	C	H
D	E	G	N	O	I	T	A	C	I	N	R	O	F
O	K	N	E	V	I	L	I	H	C	H	H	C	H
L	R	I	M	P	U	R	I	T	Y	C	N	I	C
A	E	M	E	M	P	A	S	S	I	O	N	E	T
T	U	R	T	S	U	L	T	D	E	E	R	G	A
R	U	N	C	L	E	A	N	N	E	S	S	L	W
Y	E	C	N	E	C	S	I	P	U	C	N	O	C

IMMORALITY, IMPURITY, LUST, PASSION, GREED, FORNICATION, IDOLATRY, EVIL, COVETOUSNESS, CONCUPISCENCE, UNCLEANNESS

make your Choice

I need to set my mind (affection) on things that are

_____, not on things on the _____.

What heavenly blessing can I focus my thoughts on today?

_____

TUESDAY COLOSSIANS 3:8-17

TAKE THE challenge

check it out!

When you get up and get dressed each morning, do you think about clothing your inner person as well as your outer body?

Every day I can choose to "clothe" my inner person or soul with evil or good. Below, find GODLY and UNGODLY inner clothing. Put a U (for Ungodly) or a G (for Godly) on the lines below, indicating the type of clothing it is.

___ anger	___ blasphemy	___ humility
___ wrath	___ rage	___ slander	___ mercy
___ love	___ kindness	___ ugly speech	___ malice
___ compassion	___ patience	___ gentleness	___ forgiveness
___ thankfulness	___ peace	___ dishonesty	

make your Choice

What godly clothing will I put on today? _____

_____

WEDNESDAY COLOSSIANS 3:18-4:1

TAKE THE challenge

check it out!

Is your family a place where you feel God's love and love His Word?

Match the following according to the passage:

_____ Wives

_____ Husbands

_____ Children

_____ Slaves (Employees)

_____ Masters (Employers)

_____ Fathers

A. Obey your parents.

B. Give (provide) for your servants (employees).

C. Obey your masters (bosses or employers).

D. Submit to your husbands.

E. Don't provoke or embitter your children to anger.

F. Love your wives.

make your Choice

Write one sentence about the kind of Christian family I'd like to have some day: _____

THURSDAY COLOSSIANS 4:2-6

TAKE THE challenge

check it out!

Has your dad or mom ever left for the day or gone on a trip and left you a list of instructions to follow while they're away?

Look at all the special instructions Paul leaves for the Colossian believers before closing his letter:

• v. 2 Keep on (circle one) writing / praying / weeping in an attitude of th_____.

• v. 3 Pray for us that God will _____ a _____ for us to share the mystery of Christ and the Gospel with those in prison.

• v. 5a Be wise / smart / foolish (circle one) in the way you act toward outsiders.

• v. 5b Redeem the time by using every opportunity God gives you.

• v. 6 Let your speech or conversation be filled with _____

make your Choice

Measure your prayer power below by putting an X on the line where you think you fit:

| Hardly ever pray | Pray once in a while | Pray often | Pray all day long |

TAKE THE challenge

check it out!

What friend or Christian leader encourages and uplifts you when you are down or sad?

Unscramble the names of those encouragers and friends Paul mentions in these verses.

TSUJUS __ __ __ __ __ __

MISSENUO __ __ __ __ __ __ __ __

CHUTISYC __ __ __ __ __ __ __ __

TRUCHRASAIS __ __ __ __ __ __ __ __ __ __ __

BRASBAAN __ __ __ __ __ __ __ __

make your Choice

How can I be an encouragement today to someone who's hurting or sad?

TAKE THE challenge

check it out!

Do you know anyone who's in prison?

Match the following from this passage:

_____ 1. Epaphras works hard for those in these places

_____ 2. The doctor / physician

_____ 3. One of the Colossians, a servant of Christ and a prayer-warrior

_____ 4. Sends greetings along with Luke

_____ 5. Had a church in their house

_____ 6. Told to complete or fulfill the Lord's work or ministry

A. Archippus

B. Demas

C. Nymphas

D. Epaphras

E. Luke

F. Laodicea and Hierapolis

make your Choice

The last thing Paul wanted the believers to "remember" was his _____. Did you know there are Christians today who are suffering in prison because of their faith in Christ? YES/ NO Pray for imprisoned believers in China, North Korea, Mongolia, and many Moslem nations.

217

wk. 51

chart your course

How do you **GROW?**

You've Gotta **KNOW!**

Know **WHAT?**

History? Math? SCIENCE?

The word **KNOW** or **KNOWLEDGE** is found _____ times in 2 Peter chapter 1.

WHAT do you know?

WHOM do you know?

SUNDAY   2 PETER 1:1-4

TAKE THE challenge

Where do we get what we need to KNOW and GROW?

Verse 1 - Where do we get our faith? Through the righteousness of _____

Verse 2 - Where do we get grace and peace?

_____

Verse 3 - Where do we get everything we need for life and godliness? From His divine _____

check it out!

I'm going to do everything I can to know God, including:

- ☐ Read my Bible every day
- ☐ Memorize my verses
- ☐ Take notes when my pastor preaches

make your Choice

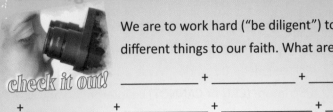

MONDAY 2 PETER 1:5-9

TAKE THE challenge

Next, we learn to ADD to what God has already given us

We are to work hard ("be diligent") to ADD seven different things to our faith. What are they?

check it out! _____ + _____ + _____

+ _____ + _____ + _____ + _____

(Make sure you know what each word means! Look it up or call your coach!)

$$4 + 4 \qquad 6 + 6 \qquad 3 + 3 \qquad 2 + 2$$

make your Choice

One of these qualities that I will work hard on today is

_____.

TUESDAY 2 PETER 1:10-14

TAKE THE challenge

How did you do with your "adding" project yesterday? Now let's find out what this hard work will do for you!

check it out!

Does all this hard work get you to heaven?

NO! But . . . .it will make you more sure of your

_____and _____ (verse 10),

which is a way of describing what it means to

be sure of your salvation.

make your Choice

Which of the following is true for you?

____ I am sure I am saved and I want to keep living that way.

____ I am not sure I am saved. I will talk to my parents or a teacher at church about this today.

219

WEDNESDAY 2 PETER 1:15-21

TAKE THE challenge

Is the Bible just a collection of stories by great authors?

Circle the correct word in each statement
Verse 16 - The accounts of Jesus **(ARE or ARE NOT)** clever, made-up stories. Verse 20 - The accounts in Scripture (CAN or CANNOT) be interpreted any way you choose. Verse 21 - Words of prophecy came from (MAN'S IDEAS or THE HOLY SPIRIT).

check it out!

make your Choice

Each day, before I read fun books or stories, I should make sure I read the _____ .

THURSDAY 2 PETER 2:1-9

TAKE THE challenge

In today's passage we find two characters from the Old Testament!

God preserved _____ (a preacher of righteousness) from the flood (v. 5).

God saved _____ (a believer living in a wicked city) from destruction (v. 7).

God saves _____ from temptations (v. 9).

check it out!

make your Choice

When I'm having a tough time, or when I'm tempted to sin, I will look to _____ to help me by praying and remembering verses that I have memorized.

FRIDAY — 2 PETER 2:10-16

check it out!

How do you treat and talk about those people God has placed over you?

Verse 10 speaks of those who have wrong desires (lust) and despise _____.

Verse 12 says that they speak evil of (or "blaspheme") things they do not _____.

Make Your Choice: I will speak of my teachers, pastor, coach, and parents only in a _____ way.

make your Choice

I will speak of my teachers, pastor, coach, and parents only in a _____ way.

SATURDAY — 2 PETER 2:17-22

TAKE THE challenge

check it out!

Did you know that we are all slaves to something?

What does verse 20 say we can escape from and then become trapped in again? _____

Verse 19 says that we are a slave to anything that controls us. What word in verse 19 means "controlled by"? _____

make your Choice

I have allowed these things to control me or use up all my time:
MUSIC - SPORTS - T.V. - FRIENDS - FOOD - VIDEO GAMES
(Circle all that apply.) I really want _____ to control me! 221

chart your course

PETER - *the most outspoken of the disciples; denied Jesus three times before His crucifixion*

JUDE - *the half-brother of Jesus; was not supportive of Jesus during his earthly ministry*

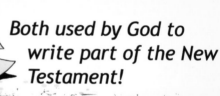

Both used by God to write part of the New Testament!

SUNDAY 2 PETER 3:1-6

TAKE THE challenge

Are you ever impatient?

These verses tell of those who are so impatient and concerned with their own desires (verse 3) that they doubt the promises of God.
What promise were they asking about in verse 4?

_____

check it out!

What judgment is described in verse 6?
(Circle the correct answer.)

    a. cast out of the Garden of Eden
    b. wandering in the wilderness
    c. the flood

make your Choice

I understand that the Lord will return to the earth to judge evil, just as He has in the past. In light of this fact, how should I live?_____

_____

Why doesn't God judge evil RIGHT NOW?

JUDGEMENT

To God, 1000 years is like _____ (v. 8).

God waits because He doesn't want anyone to

_____, but wants everyone to

_____ (v. 9). Someday the earth will

be destroyed with _____ (v. 10).

make your Choice

Thank you, God, for Your patience with me
-- *giving me time to repent!*

How should we live while we look forward to Heaven?

Peter tells those he is writing to that if they are

looking for Christ's return, they will be diligent

(make every effort) to be found in Christ:

(1) _____,

(2) _____ and

(3) _____ (v.?)

make your Choice

How do I want Jesus to find me when He returns? _____

_____

_____

223

WEDNESDAY JUDE 1-7

Why do we need to fight to defend the faith?

According to verse four, what kind of men had secretly slipped into the church? _____ men They wanted to turn God's _____ into immorality. What did they deny? _____
_____

Whom did God destroy (v. 5)? Those who did not
_____

make your Choice

I must always compare what people say to what God says (in the _____).

THURSDAY JUDE 8-11

Are you strong enough to resist the devil by yourself?

Who was Michael? The a_____

Who was he fighting against? _____

Who did he ask to rebuke his enemy? _____

make your Choice

Is what I want more important to me than seeing what someone else needs? YES/ NO Whom will I choose to put ahead of myself today? _____

224

FRIDAY JUDE 12-19

check it out!

What causes you to complain?

"Walking after your own lusts" means thinking only about what YOU want. What kind of talk does this attitude bring out? (Circle each correct choice)

Thankful? Grumbling? Finding Fault? Praising the good? Humble?

make your Choice

Is what I want more important to me than seeing what someone else needs? YES/ NO Whom will I choose to put ahead of myself today? _____

SATURDAY JUDE 20-25

check it out!

Are you interested in your friend's relationship with God?

In verses 20 and 21, who are you to build up with faith and prayer?_____

In verses 22 and 23, whose spiritual life are you to be concerned about?_____

In verse 24, what is Christ able to do for you?

_____

make your Choice

I will _____ every day to help myself grow closer to God. A friend that I can encourage in his/her Christian growth is

_____.

225

chart your course

RUTH: *friendship*
GLEANING: *gathering or picking up leftovers*
KINSMAN: *relative*

FAMINE: *no food*

MARA: *bitter*

NAOMI: *pleasant*

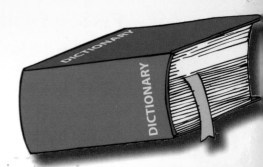

DICTIONARY

SUNDAY   RUTH 1:1-14

TAKE THE challenge

check it out!

The cast of characters!

Pretend that this passage is a play and that you need to discover what happens to the cast of characters. What happens to each of the following characters in this passage? Use the verse "clues" to help you: Elimelech - husband and father - _____ v. 3 Mahlon - son and husband - _____ v. 5 Chilion - son and husband - _____ v.5 Naomi - wife and mother - _____ v.6 Orpah (not "Oprah") - wife and daughter-in-law - _____ vv. 11 and 14 Ruth - Stay tuned to find out what happens to her tomorrow!

make your Choice

Sometimes things in my life are hard - like moving to a new place, the death of a loved one, a pet dying, a friend moving away, divorced parents, trouble at school, or illness. Have any of these things happened to me in the last year? _____ (Circle it.) As a believer, Who can I depend on in hard times? _____

MONDAY RUTH 1:15-22

TAKE THE challenge

check it out!

Don't make me go!

_____ is Naomi's daughter-in-law. _____ has decided to return to her homeland, because she has heard that the famine has ended. Naomi wants Ruth to go _____ (v. 15), but Ruth doesn't want to go! Where does she want to go? _____ _____ (v. 16) Check out Chart Your Course to see what Naomi's name means and what "Mara" (the name she wants to be called when she returns) means. Why do you think that she wants to be called "Mara"? See v. 21:_____

make your Choice

Ruth must have seen something in Naomi that made her want to know Naomi's God better. Who in my life shows me Jesus and makes me want to know Him better? _____
I will take time to thank God right now for this person.

TUESDAY RUTH 2:1-12

TAKE THE challenge

check it out!

Hungry? Go gleaning!

God provided a way for poor people to get food during Bible times. It is called gleaning. (See Chart Your Course.) Whose field did Ruth "happen" to go to? _____ (v. 3) Who was Boaz, according to verse 1?_____
What had Boaz heard about Ruth in v. 11? _____

_____

_____

_____

make your Choice

Boaz had heard amazing things about Ruth from others. What might others say about me? **LOUD – PUSHY – UNKIND – CARING – LOYAL – HONEST – SILLY – TROUBLE MAKER – ENCOURAGING – LEADER – DISHONEST** *Please Jesus, help me to conquer this.* 227

WEDNESDAY RUTH 2:13-23

TAKE THE challenge

check it out!

A sweet set-up!

When Naomi heard where _____ had been gleaning for the day, she was thrilled because _____ was a relative of hers. She told Ruth to stay in Boaz's fields all the time! Unscramble the puzzle tiles below to find out what was provided to Ruth because she stayed only in Boaz's fields.

N TIO PRO TEC

_____

make your Choice

God has set up areas of protection in my life as well. Who are the people I should listen to who only want the best for me? (List all you can think of.)_____

_____

THURSDAY RUTH 3:1-18

TAKE THE challenge

check it out!

A strange plan - an obedient daughter-in-law!

Write down the steps Naomi asked Ruth to take for the plan she devised in verses 3 and 4:

Step 1 - Wash_____

Step 2 – Put _____

Step 3 – Go_____

Step 4 – Wait until _____

Step 5 – Uncover_____

This plan seems strange to us today, but this was the way that Ruth could let Boaz, as a close relative, know that she would like him to marry her and take care of Naomi and her.

make your Choice

Even though this plan was strange, Ruth trusted Naomi and was willing to do what Naomi asked without questioning, complaining, or grumbling. How would my mom say I doing in the obedience category?

_____

228

FRIDAY — RUTH 4:1-12

TAKE THE challenge
check it out!

Will you marry her?
No, here's my shoe!

Boaz was not the closest relative to Naomi . . . .
There was one man who was a closer relative.
Where did Boaz meet that relative?_____
How many other men did he ask to be witnesses?___
What did Boaz ask the man if he wanted to buy?
_____ What else would the man have to do after buying the
___d?_____ What did the man do to show
__at the deal was sealed?_____

make your Choice

Boaz, a man of wealth and power, chose to marry Ruth, a poor
foreigner, to save Naomi and her from a life of hardship, pain,
and shame. He was their kinsman-redeemer! Do I have a
Redeemer from sin and death to call my own? YES / NO
Who is it? ___ ___ ___ ___ ___

SATURDAY — RUTH 4:13-22

TAKE THE challenge
check it out!

A grandson for Naomi . . .
a great-grandfather for David!

Boaz and Ruth got married and had a son, whom
they named _____. Obed became the
grandfather of the great king David! Find the
secret word in the puzzle below to discover what
special person descended from David's line.

make your Choice

God knows the plans He has for me in my future. I can't see it, but He
knows all about it. I will write one dream for my future here
_____. *Lord God, I pray that
You will take my dreams for the future and do something great in my life.
I give all my dreams and plans to You and trust You with my future!*

229

WORD OF LIFE
Weekly Quiet Time Passage

So that all club and family members will be on the same passages, the following dates correspond to the weekly passages. These dates are used for all Word of Life Quiet Times and daily radio broadcasts.

Week 1	Aug 24 – Aug 30	Psalms 51:1-56:13
Week 2	Aug 31 – Sep 6	Psalms 57:1-63:11
Week 3	Sep 7 – Sep 13	Psalms 64:1-68:35
Week 4	Sep 14 – Sep 20	Psalms 69:1-72:11
Week 5	Sep 21 – Sep 27	Psalms 72:12-76:12
Week 6	Sep 28 – Oct 4	1 Timothy 1:1-4:8
Week 7	Oct 5 – Oct 11	1 Timothy 4:9-6:21
Week 8	Oct 12 – Oct 18	Leviticus 1:1-23:14
Week 9	Oct 19 – Oct 25	Leviticus 23:15-26:46
Week 10	Oct 26 – Nov 1	Mark 1:1-3:12
Week 11	Nov 2 – Nov 8	Mark 3:13-5:20
Week 12	Nov 9 – Nov 15	Mark 5:21-7:13
Week 13	Nov 16 – Nov 22	Mark 7:14-9:29
Week 14	Nov 23 – Nov 29	Mark 9:30-11:11
Week 15	Nov 30 – Dec 6	Mark 11:12-13:23
Week 16	Dec 7 – Dec 13	Mark 13:24-14:65
Week 17	Dec 14 – Dec 20	Mark 14:66-16:20
Week 18	Dec 21 – Dec 27	1 John 1:1-2:27
Week 19	Dec 28 – Jan 3	1 John 2:28-4:21
Week 20	Jan 4 – Jan 10	1 John 5:1 - 3 John 14
Week 21	Jan 11 – Jan 17	Ezra 1:1-5:5
Week 22	Jan 18 – Jan 24	Ezra 5:6-8:26
Week 23	Jan 25 – Jan 31	Ezra 9:1 - Haggai 2:23
Week 24	Feb 1 – Feb 7	Nehemiah 1:1-4:23
Week 25	Feb 8 – Feb 14	Nehemiah 5:1-13:14
Week 26	Feb 15 – Feb 21	Acts 1:1-3:11
Week 27	Feb 22 – Feb 28	Acts 3:12-5:32
Week 28	Mar 1 – Mar 7	Acts 5:33-8:13
Week 29	Mar 8 – Mar 14	Acts 8:14-10:8
Week 30	Mar 15 – Mar 21	Acts 10:9-12:25
Week 31	Mar 22 – Mar 28	Acts 13:1-15:12
Week 32	Mar 29 – Apr 4	Acts 15:13-17:21
Week 33	Apr 5 – Apr 11	Acts 17:22-20:12
Week 34	Apr 12 – Apr 18	Acts 20:13-22:30
Week 35	Apr 19 – Apr 25	Acts 23:1-25:27
Week 36	Apr 26 – May 2	Acts 26:1-28:31
Week 37	May 3 – May 9	Numbers 1:1-8:18
Week 38	May 10 – May 16	Numbers 8:19-13:25
Week 39	May 17 – May 23	Numbers 13:26-20:12
Week 40	May 24 – May 30	Numbers 20:23-35:25
Week 41	May 31 – Jun 6	Galatians 1:1-3:9
Week 42	Jun 7 – Jun 13	Galatians 3:10-5:1
Week 43	Jun 14 – Jun 20	Galatians 5:2-6:18
Week 44	Jun 21 – Jun 27	Proverbs 11:1-13:13
Week 45	Jun 28 – Jul 4	Proverbs 13:14-15:33
Week 46	Jul 5 – Jul 11	1 Thessalonians 1:1-3:13
Week 47	Jul 12 – Jul 18	1 Thessalonians 4:1-5:28
Week 48	Jul 19 – Jul 25	2 Thessalonians 1:1-3:18
Week 49	Jul 26 – Aug 1	Colossians 1:1-2:15
Week 50	Aug 2 – Aug 8	Colossians 2:16-4:18
Week 51	Aug 9 – Aug 15	2 Peter 1:1-2:22
Week 52	Aug 16 – Aug 22	2 Peter 3:1 - Jude 25
Week 53	Aug 23 – Aug 29	Ruth 1:1-4:22